PRAISE FOR

A CANCER WARRIOR

"Dusty's story is one of bravery in the face of adversity. After receiving a grim cancer diagnosis in September 2020, Dusty could have easily gone into freeze or flight mode. Instead, he gathered up his A team, leaned hard into his faith, and fought one of the toughest battles of his life! In A Cancer Warrior: How I Fought and Survived My Battle with Pancreatic Cancer, *Dusty offers up his personal experiences with pancreatic cancer and shares the framework that worked for him and his family. If you know someone who is battling cancer, this is a hopeful story worth sharing."*

—JONNY IMERMAN, Co-Founder of Imerman Angels

"Seconds after Dusty Mysen received the devastating news he had been diagnosed with pancreatic cancer, his perception of time (and life's priorities!) changed in a single moment. In this beautifully written and heartfelt memoir, Dusty shares his remarkable and inspiring fight to defeat this terrible disease. How did Dusty navigate the storm? He chose to fight and not become a statistic. Dusty is not a victim of cancer, he's a survivor!

Choosing a warrior's mentality, Dusty was determined to defy the odds. This is an inspiring book about one man's unrelenting human spirit. It's about faith, family, courage, and hope—and how you can face adversity head on to overcome obstacles!"

**—TIM ALLEN, Executive Associate Assistant Director,
University of Central Florida**

"I love Dusty's six-part framework for fighting cancer. He focused on 'Faith over Fear' to make his plan actionable, and I plan to apply his framework to my own life with respect to overcoming my own challenges. Through his story, Dusty teaches us that by being vulnerable and inviting others into the battle with you, you don't have to go through it alone. Too many times in life we suffer in silence out of pride or masculinity. Dusty's story showed me how powerful we can be when we can accept support."

—DEAN BRODY, Founder and CEO, REVEL Moments

"This book was written with unsparing honesty and emotional truths. Dusty's pancreatic cancer diagnosis came as a complete shock to me and his friends, and over a three-year period, we watched an unbelievable series of challenges unfold for him and his family. Ultimately, Dusty's story is an uplifting reminder for all of us to stay focused on what is most important in our lives. To say he and his family are "beating the odds" is a complete understatement—Dusty is not just alive, he's living a life that's thriving!"

—CLAYTON BILL, Director, Indiana Trust Wealth Management

"Wow, just wow! Thank you for writing this book, Dusty. It has blessed me, and I believe the Lord will use it to bless and guide countless others. You are courageous to share such personal and intimate details of your journey. Your transparency, resiliency, and faith are humbling. Your words will help anyone facing cancer, and really, any challenge this life may bring. You are a champion for hope and your words will inspire and encourage others to persevere. I can't wait to share this book with people who need to know they are not alone. This book is for those who need to push through just one more day, for those who need to believe that they can be healed and who need to know that it's ok to ask for help. This book is for those who need to know someone who has gone through this hell—and survived. You are the light of hope for a new day!"

—GINA KELL SPEHN, Co-Founder/President at New Day Foundation, *NY Times* bestselling author and TEDx speaker

"A riveting read on one man's fight for survival with practical takeaways to help anyone that is going through serious life challenges. This is a must read and inspiring story of faith over fear!"

—RICH LOHMAN, Founder and Head Coach, Project 12:02

A
CANCER
WARRIOR

A
CANCER
WARRIOR

HOW I FOUGHT AND SURVIVED MY BATTLE WITH PANCREATIC CANCER

DUSTY MYSEN

RESILIENT JOURNEY, LLC
METAMORA, MICHIGAN, UNITED STATES

For Katie, Tristen, Landon, Parker, and Grady.
You guys are my everything.

CONTENTS

Proverbs 3:5-6: *"Trust in the Lord with all your heart, and lean not on your own understanding. In all your ways submit to Him, and He will make your paths straight."*

INTRODUCTION

"Mr. Mysen, I'm sorry to have to tell you this, but you have pancreatic cancer. In my expert opinion, it's non-operable. There's not much that can be done."

That was the simple and concise, yet utterly soul-crushing, diagnosis a surgeon delivered to me on September 22, 2020, following a biopsy of a mass in my pancreas. It was the news that completely changed the course of my life, the statement that changed everything.

At just forty-seven years old I had been given the equivalent of a death sentence. I couldn't even comprehend the magnitude of what I'd just learned. All I could think was, *How in the hell did I end up here?*

Being diagnosed with inoperable pancreatic cancer at such a young age was not something I thought would be on the bingo card of my life. Yet there I was, thrown headlong and unwillingly into life as a cancer patient. I quickly realized that role would become all-encompassing, a full-time job of sorts. It became my identity. I was no longer the Dusty Mysen of my previous forty-six years of life. I was now Dusty Mysen, the guy with pancreatic cancer. My cancer was now at the forefront of all I did, of everything I was.

Prior to my diagnosis, I was many things. I was an extreme extrovert, the ultimate people person, someone who built strong relationships at every opportunity. I had a thriving career, one in which I was a respected leader. I was an athlete and someone who loved to get in the gym on a regular basis. I was an extreme competitor in every aspect of my life. I was a coach, strongly focused on teaching life lessons to the kids in our community through sports. I was a Christian. I was, above all other things, a devoted husband and father. I was all that and much more.

Being diagnosed with cancer changed all of that. I was still those things, but each of those other portions of my identity was now fully intertwined with the new cancer part of me. The cancer had rooted itself into my life in every way. It felt as if the cancer was trying to overpower the rest of me. But it ultimately only amplified and enhanced who I already was.

The relationships I had so enjoyed building were now even more important, as the support of those around me became critical to my survival. I had to lean on the people in my life to an extent I had never experienced before. The battle I was in was simply too big to fight alone. That ultimately made me want to give back to them with the same level of intensity. Having cancer allowed me to deepen those relationships. Being so sick and having to face my own mortality allowed me to open up so much more. Not only did I need to lean on my close family and friends, but after my diagnosis I also had to trust a large team of doctors and medical professionals with my life. I added them to the army of people who were such a significant part of my existence.

My career became more than just a way to pay the bills; I realized it was a critical part of my identity that I was determined to not let the cancer take away. Work became an invaluable tool to escape the cancer, a place where I could still add real value and not just be a struggling cancer patient.

The athlete and competitor in me shifted direction from men's league sports and an emphasis on fitness to a single-minded focus on fighting for my life. I was facing the biggest and toughest adversary imaginable, fighting my own Goliath in the form of my cancer.

Cancer didn't take that part of who I was; it only magnified it. My battle transitioned that part of me to the status of cancer warrior, an identity I grew to take great pride in and lean into completely.

The pre-cancer version of me was a Christian who was slowly learning to walk in my faith. My diagnosis quickly forced that walk into a run. I had to lean fully into my faith. I had to use it continuously and consistently in an effort to not let the cancer overpower me.

Finally, the cancer completely intertwined with my role as a family man, a husband, and a father. The cancer didn't just try to overpower me; it also tried to overpower my entire family. Cancer made me fully appreciate the importance of my family in my life. It made everything I did family-focused. I was fighting to beat it for them, to stay alive for them, to leave a legacy for them.

My cancer didn't replace who I already was. It didn't become me. It instead forced me to further grow, to rely on the best parts of the person I'd always been. In the end, after a long and challenging battle, it ultimately made me a better version of myself.

Battling cancer taught me so much. It forced me to dig deep and develop an approach to fight the monster that I was forced to face. It was too big a challenge to manage without a game plan. Shortly after my diagnosis, I developed my personal strategy for my fight.

As I struggled through those first few months, I figured out what worked for me in the battle with cancer. I ultimately settled on six main components that I felt were critical for me in my fight.

1. Faith.
2. A positive attitude.
3. A focus on what I was fighting for.
4. Fitness and my physical health.
5. A strong support system.
6. Advocating for my own health plan.

I learned to lean on those six pillars completely, and they helped me with each and every hardship cancer threw at me. They became the foundation for my battle, like the playbooks I had learned in sports in my youth. When I felt I could not go on, I forced myself to focus on these areas, and they always pulled me right back into the fight.

I learned that my strategy wasn't just a valuable tool in fighting cancer; it was one I could apply to all the challenges life could throw at me.

The life-and-death fight that being diagnosed with cancer threw me into ultimately gave me a new perspective and purpose in my life. It showed how much of a fighter I truly was. It taught me that the grit, positivity, and faith I exhibited throughout the battle could be inspiring and motivating to others. Through my struggles, I could become a positive light for people in need.

As I learned what my story could do for others, using my experiences through cancer to give back became my purpose. I want to use my story to inspire, to motivate, and, most importantly, to give a little hope to someone who can really use it. Cancer forced me into the fight. I didn't get a choice. But how I faced it *was* my choice. And how I use the lessons it taught me is also a choice. And I choose to use my battle to help others at every opportunity.

CHAPTER 1

LIFE BEFORE THE CANCER

Until my cancer diagnosis, I had lived a very blessed life.

I was born on August 1, 1973, in Muskegon, Michigan, which is this cool little beach town along the shores of Lake Michigan. Growing up there offered a nice combination of beach-town vibes and the tight-knit culture of a small Midwest community. I was always outdoors with family and friends, enjoying all the area had to offer. We spent our days boating, swimming, playing sports, and at the beaches of Lake Michigan.

I have a brother, Ryan, who's three-and-a-half years younger than me. My parents, Dan and Cindy, raised us in a closely connected community with lots of cousins and family close by. We grew up living the American dream. We were middle-class, and by no means wealthy, but I couldn't have asked for anything more from my years growing up in Muskegon.

We were a very close family. No matter how hectic our schedules were, family dinners with all four of us gathered around the dining room table were the norm. Our close family bond spread beyond the four of us to our extended family as well, and our weekends were frequently filled with large family get-togethers with my grandparents, aunts and uncles, and cousins.

We lived on the outside of town, and we had a very large yard where our neighborhood friends frequently gathered to hang out. We played endless games of football, baseball, soccer, and other sports and outside activities.

Sports were the central focus of my childhood. As a kid, I played organized football, basketball, baseball, soccer, and hockey. Our family was at a field or ice rink pretty much every night of the week, all year round. Outside of school, my time was fully consumed by an endless string of practices and games. I never complained about the hectic schedule. I loved every second of it, and on those fields and rinks was exactly where I wanted to be. Competing in sports was my biggest passion, and the focal point of almost everything in my young life.

I was super-competitive as a child and remained so as an adult. All I ever wanted to do was compete. That was true in sports, as well as in school and everywhere else. Competitiveness was, and probably still is, my most defining trait. A board game between my brother and me could quickly turn into a fierce battle.

I had no idea how valuable that competitiveness would eventually become, when my biggest battle would arise.

My parents, who both worked full time, always found a way to adjust their busy schedules to ensure we made it to our many practices and games. As kids, we were oblivious to the sacrifices they made to give us such amazing childhoods. I now realize just how lucky we were and have made every effort to follow in my parents' footsteps, ensuring my kids have the opportunity to do everything they want as well.

My focus on sports and academics carried me through my high school years at Muskegon's Reeths-Puffer High School. I focused on hockey at first, eventually shifting to wrestling and baseball, while running cross-country as a training tool. I was pretty good at wrestling, eventually setting my school's record for most career wins—a record my brother broke a few years later. I also pitched and played first base on the varsity baseball team.

The lessons I learned during my participation in both team and individual sports were critical in preparing me for all the challenges life would eventually throw at me. Team sports taught me how to be a good teammate, how to perform a specific role to the best of my ability, how to build the relationships and bonds necessary for success, and how to be a strong leader. Individual sports taught me about being accountable, the value of individual hard work and training, and how to deal with the pressures of being alone in the spotlight. The combination of team and individual sports in my youth lay the foundation for the rest of my life.

When I faced the challenges of getting everyone on the same page for a difficult group project in college, I leaned on the methods I'd developed as a leader on my wrestling, hockey, and baseball teams. The same lessons were also invaluable when I was first promoted to a managerial role in my career. I was able to lead due to my strong relationship-building skills, my ability to motivate, and my focus on leading by example.

I leaned on my sports training when stepping on stage to give presentations to management or critical customers. I had learned to thrive by not letting the pressure of the moment bother me, and instead trusting in the endless hours of training I had put in to prepare for that moment. That life lesson was carried over into every management presentation or critical customer interaction of my career. I prepared diligently and trusted in that preparation to allow me to shine in the spotlight.

Finally, all those experiences and lessons learned on the fields, rinks, and mats of my youth lay the foundation for the skillset I would need in my eventual battle with cancer. I was able to see cancer as just another opponent. It was the fiercest adversary I would ever face, but the strategy and methods needed to compete against that monster were no different from what I'd used in all those games and matches. Sports mirror life, and conversely, life mirrors sports. Sports prepared me for all that life would throw my way.

I did well academically through high school, finishing seventh in my class of roughly 250 students. My academic successes gave me multiple options for college. But my most important take-aways from my middle school and high school years were the incredible friendships I was able to make, many of which I still hold to this day.

The incredibly close bonds that I built with my core group of friends in school became the foundation of my support system for life. By the time we were in high school, we were together all the time. My parents used to joke that I stayed at friends' houses more often than I slept in my own bed. Their parents became like additional parents for me, and my parents the same to them.

We even joined each other for family holidays. One of my closest friends, Alistair, was born in Scotland. Christmas evenings at his parents' house were some of my favorite times. After I spent the day with my family at my maternal and paternal grandparents' homes, I headed to spend Christmas evening with his family. I learned and grew to love all their Scottish holiday traditions and even acquired a taste for good Scotch whisky at a younger-than-normal age.

My relationship with Alistair and the rest of our friend group went beyond friendship; it was more like a brotherhood. We shared everything. We were there for each other through every teenage challenge, and because of that, the connection we all developed was abnormally strong and has lasted a lifetime.

I never took those relationships for granted. That type of bond is rare. That group of guys built a foundation of support that I would continue to rely on through my entire life, including when my cancer reared its ugly head.

As that close group of friends and I finished high school, I had some opportunities to wrestle at a few different colleges but decided to pass on those and attend my dream school, Michigan State University, to focus on academics instead.

My dad had gone to MSU, and I grew up bleeding green and white. Even though I had friends who also went on to Michigan State, we all decided to have roommates randomly assigned to us that freshman year. While rooming with an existing friend would have been the safe approach, the idea of meeting new and different people and spreading our wings a little appealed to all of us. Building relationships is one of my favorite things, and college seemed like the perfect place to do just that.

This turned out to be one of the best decisions of my young life. While I stayed close with those friends from high school, and we frequently hung out together, my randomly assigned roommates and floormates exposed me to a whole new group. The guys I met and roomed with that first year at MSU ended up being my roommates throughout college and have remained my closest friends. Clayton, Joel, Matt, Seamus, and I faced that massive life change together, and that bonded us quickly and tightly.

My new friendships also gave me an outlet for my never-ending competitive nature, as they were very similar to me and always up for an excessively spirited contest with the occasional wager involved. Not long into our freshman year, we were regularly battling it out at tennis, racquetball, basketball, or any other competition we could think of. Beer was usually our wager of choice (usually cheap beer). And just to make sure they don't forget as they read this, I am 100 percent sure that I won far more of those bets than I lost!

Our ongoing competitions and bets carried over long after college, as we continued to meet up for intense battles on the golf course for many years to come. At least in our post-college years the quality of beverages we wagered with improved significantly.

After spending four-and-a-half fun-filled and academically challenging years on that beautiful campus with those incredible friends, I graduated with my bachelor's degree in December 1995.

I took a position as an electrical engineer in the automotive industry in Saginaw, Michigan. I learned the engineering ropes there for just over three years, and then took another engineering opportunity in the Detroit suburbs. I learned what aspects of the industry I truly enjoyed, which helped set the path for all my future career moves. My extroverted nature and my strong desire to be a leader eventually took me away from engineering and into the management and sales side of the business. As I shifted positions and advanced in my career, I was able to smoothly transition into roles that utilized both my engineering education and my strongest personality traits.

I spent the next twenty-plus years at my second employer in various roles, climbing through the ranks. I was an engineering supervisor, then a project manager, a sales manager, and then an executive director of sales. I was able to work my way up in a field that never grew boring for me and that I was able to excel in. I loved cars and technology, so I had definitely picked the correct industry. It's a blessing to find a career that truly fits your skillset as well as your interests. I've been extremely lucky.

My career has also given me amazing opportunities to travel all around the world, meet many amazing people, and experience many different cultures. I've dined in a traditional Chinese restaurant on the seventy-fifth floor of a skyscraper in Shanghai. I've worked and traveled throughout Germany, enjoying the country's people, food, and beer. I've also had the pleasure of enjoying the architecture and amazing food of northern Italy while on business trips there. My trips to South America were always enlightening. Tel Aviv, Israel, became one of my favorite cities in the world over my many trips there. Traveling taught me so much about the world, and I built relationships far and wide.

Even with my busy career, I found some time for hobbies. I retained my competitive streak and love of sports, so I continued to find ways to stay in the game. I played men's beer league hockey and loved it. I also played men's league basketball as an adult. My overly competitive nature wouldn't allow me to just participate in sports for the fun of it; I had to be good. I had to win. This forced me to stay in shape to keep up with, and continue to beat, the younger guys I played against. Finding time to continue my sports and hobbies as my career progressed kept me balanced. It gave me something beyond just my professional life to focus on and to expend some of my vast amounts of energy. At that point in life, during my mid-to-late twenties, my plate was completely full with my growing career, my sports and hobbies, and spending time with friends.

· · ·

After college, that close group of hometown friends had all settled in various cities, mostly around Michigan. I spent almost every weekend traveling to their apartments to hang out together as a group. It was rare that we went more than a few weeks without seeing each other.

As we had exited college and started into the next phase of life, many of my friends were settling down and getting married. The wedding parties were always the same, that same core group of tight-knit friends who had been together nonstop since middle school. I stood up in over ten weddings and was the best man in three of them. The bond of our friendship, our brotherhood, meant that we all had to be a part of each other's biggest life milestones (and led to me renting a lot of tuxedos).

As my friends were settling down and getting married, I didn't feel a need to change anything. I wasn't close to being ready for that stage of life yet. But then I met Katie, and everything changed.

· · ·

Way back in May of 2002, a friend asked me to go on a blind date with his girlfriend's friend. I normally wouldn't say yes to something like that, but for some unknown reason I talked myself into giving it a try on this occasion. The four of us met up at a restaurant in Saginaw, Michigan, had some dinner, and went out for drinks after. I was twenty-eight years old, and completely unaware that one night in Saginaw could change a man's life forever.

I wasn't focused on finding a serious relationship. I'd had girlfriends in the past, but leading up to meeting Katie, I was happily focused on everything but a relationship. Don't get me wrong, I'd always hoped and planned to settle down and have a family at some point, but I felt strongly that it wasn't that time for me yet. With everything falling perfectly together in all the other aspects of my life, I didn't feel like I needed a serious romantic relationship at that time. All that quickly changed after I met Katie on that blind date.

Blind dates in 2002 were truly blind. You couldn't do a quick social media check pre-date to see what you were about to get into. The only way we could learn about someone new was through good old-fashioned word-of-mouth from someone in the know. Unfortunately, my friend who set me up on that date had also never met Katie, so he wasn't much help in preparing me before the date. That made the whole event a little scary.

Not to be deterred, I developed a plan. At the time, the Detroit Red Wings were about to start an NHL playoff series. My friend and I were both hockey fans. So, I developed a hockey-related rating system of sorts to give me an indication of what to expect before I showed up at that restaurant to meet Katie.

The plan went as follows: On the way to Saginaw, I would call my friend who had already planned to arrive a little earlier than me. At the point I called, he would have met her and talked to her a little. Not a lot to work with, but enough to give me a positive report before arriving, or potentially enough to tell me to fake an illness and turn the car around and rush home!

Our rating system was based on a seven-game hockey series. I would call and ask him how he thought the Red Wings were going to do in the upcoming series. If my friend thought that I would find Katie attractive and she seemed nice (and normal), he would respond that he thought the Red Wings would win the series in anywhere from four to seven games—four being the best. If he thought it wasn't going to be a good match, he'd respond that he thought the Red Wings were going to lose the series.

When I made the call on that old flip phone, he quickly responded with an answer of, "I think the Red Wings will win in five games." That quick response was all I needed. She had a positive review, and I was ready to meet her and enjoy the date. I kept driving north, and quickly joined them at the restaurant. (For the record, in hindsight he was wrong, Katie is definitely a "Red Wings win in *four*!")

After that first blind date at her favorite Mexican restaurant, I knew almost immediately that she was the one for me. We started seriously dating right after, and I was all in. But I wasn't just dating Katie; she had a two-year-old son, Tristen, so I was getting a package deal. Once I met Tristen a few weeks after that first date, I was certain I was all in on both of them. Things sure can turn around quickly. I went from being a twenty-eight-year-old single guy, focused completely on my career and having fun, to suddenly being ready for a relationship that came with a two-year-old.

People have asked me how I could have shifted my perspective so quickly and completely, and the only answer I have is that when you know deep down in your heart that she is *the one*—that they are *the ones*—you grab on tight and don't let them go. So that's exactly what I did.

I proposed to Katie on Christmas Eve in 2003. We were in my living room, sitting by the Christmas tree when I popped the question. Tristen, who was supposed to be sleeping upstairs, had decided he needed to participate too.

When I asked her that very important question, she fortunately said yes. Actually, she initially responded with a shocked, "Are you f'n kidding me?" but then asked for a redo and gave a clear and loving answer of "YES!" After I slid the engagement ring onto her finger, I saw Tristen peek his little head around the corner with a big smile, and he asked me a very important question: "Does this mean I can call you Daddy now?" Those were the best gifts I could have received that holiday season. From that night on I was Daddy, and then eventually just Dad as I watched him grow older.

Our life as a family of three was off and running. We were married in Katie's Brown City church on October 23, 2004. Although our wedding day was overcast and rainy, it was the perfect day to us, with all our family and friends in attendance. Hearing her say "I do" during our small wedding ceremony felt like the most important milestone of my life. I was gaining my ideal partner. The wedding was followed by a fun-filled night of dancing and partying with the people we loved—the perfect kickoff for my new life with the loves of my life.

After our honeymoon week in Mexico, Katie and I jumped right into married life. My career was progressing. She was early in her career as a nurse, while continuing her education toward an advanced nursing degree. Tristen was starting kindergarten. Shortly after our marriage, I officially adopted Tristen, formalizing our already strong father-son relationship. It was the final step, although just a formality in my opinion, to solidify our little family. All was going perfectly, and absolutely nothing like what I thought was in store for my life's plans just a few years prior.

We began to add to our family. Our son Landon arrived in August 2005, our daughter Parker in May 2008, and finally our son Grady, who was born in August 2012. Who knew that one little blind date back in 2002 would lead to the family of my dreams? God definitely blesses us in awesome and unexpected ways.

CHAPTER 2

A FAMILY MAN
ABOVE EVERYTHING ELSE

Family is everything to me. Growing up with what my parents modeled for me . . . well, there was no other choice.

Once I became a father, my focus shifted fully to the kids and Katie. While I loved my job, hobbies, and sports, everything else took a back seat to being a parent and a husband. Even all the little things about family life brought me so much joy. The kids' giggles and laughter, their funny little comments, and their never-ending questions and curiosity made me extremely happy.

I quickly settled into the daily activities of parenthood—from those early days of feedings and diaper changes to the later days of being a homework assistant and taxi driver. I was their biggest fan, also stepping into the role of their teams' coach in many cases. I tried my best to do it all.

Katie and I were able to figure out the right balance as co-parents and worked as a solid team in our parental roles. It wasn't always easy or perfect, but we always faced the challenges together as a team. We agreed early on to equally share in the many responsibilities that parenthood added to our lives. Trying to balance both of our busy careers with the kids' schedules was hectic and sometimes put a strain on things. I'm sure there were times, when my career required me to be away frequently on business trips, that Katie felt our split in parental responsibilities was not so balanced. But in those times, she always carried the extra burden and kept the family running smoothly until I could get home. Like most working families, we persevered and grew stronger together over time.

I saw my own childhood memories playing out in front of me through my own family. My favorite activities I enjoyed as a kid were now events I could share with them. I loved our weekends together at the lake, where we'd spend our time boating and swimming. Or when we loaded up the entire family and hit the road, headed out to their sports tournaments in and around the Midwest.

Some of my fondest memories are of the annual family vacations we took together. One of my favorite trips was the week we spent in the Ozarks. This was back in 2017, and it ranks high on Katie's list too. Our whole family, plus Katie's parents, siblings, and our nieces and nephews rented a houseboat. There were sixteen of us living on one boat together for an entire week. While this may have been a little too much togetherness for some, that was not the case for us. We spent the days cruising around the enormous lake, swimming, fishing, and lying under the hot sun, always together.

To this day, our kids still retell their stories from the houseboat. That trip was special for me because it was exactly the kind of togetherness I grew up with in my own family. My parents, brother, and I would spend weeks completely isolated from others on camping trips, just the four of us. Those trips were foundational for me building out my own family experiences and will stay with me throughout my entire life.

•   •   •

In many ways, my four kids are quite similar to each other, and to me and Katie as well. They're all good students, they're all very social, and they each have their own amazing group of friends. Of course, sports are also important to each of them. We got them started early, and because of that, sports became a primary focal point for our entire family.

Our family schedule is arranged around their practices, games, and tournaments. Katie and I have become master schedulers. Our weekends and family trips consist of endless amounts of cross-country races and basketball, volleyball, and lacrosse tournaments in cities around Michigan and the Midwest. We attend them together as a family, supporting each person along the way.

Katie and I love each of our kids' own unique traits.

Tristen, our oldest, is a natural leader and role model for his siblings. He sometimes acts as a third parent around our house, and he's very focused on keeping the family close together. He is always the intermediary and voice of reason when the other kids start to argue.

Landon is unquestionably a second child. He is extremely independent, always doing things his own way. Easygoing, he doesn't stress and takes things as they come. He has an incredible sense of humor and is amazingly strong and resilient.

Parker, our only daughter, is creative and artistic. She's an advocate for anyone in need, showing great care for every person or animal she encounters.

Grady is our youngest, but as the fourth child, he is quite mature for his age. He's an absolute daredevil, afraid of nothing. He's extremely social with kids and adults and is following directly in the footsteps of his extroverted father.

Being able to look into four young sets of eyes and seeing yourself reflected back is one of the greatest experiences in the world.

When I eventually faced my battle with cancer, those four sets of eyes, five when you added Katie's, would become my complete focus. They were what I fought for. They were my reason to battle. My kids were amazing young mirrors of Katie and me, but they were not yet fully developed into who they each would ultimately become. They still had so much growing and learning to do. I had to fight with everything in my being to stick around to see the completion of that process, to experience it with Katie, the love of my life, and to not leave her to manage it alone.

CHAPTER 3

GETTING HEALTHY AND TRYING TO STAY YOUNG DURING A PANDEMIC

In late February of 2020, as the first whispers of COVID-19 were emerging in the United States, Katie and I had a quick four-day trip planned to a resort in Mexico. We needed a break from freezing our butts off in our dark Michigan winter, as many people from our region of the country do in the middle of the season. It was a great little break from the reality of our hectic careers and the cold weather, and unbeknownst to us at the time, was the last hurrah before all hell broke loose with the pandemic.

I was forty-six years old at the time and, like nearly everyone else, had never lived through anything remotely like it. That year, the entire world was unexpectedly stopped in its tracks. It would also be the beginning of the most challenging chapter of my life health-wise. The craziness of that time was about to intertwine itself, in both good ways and bad, with what was about to be the most difficult journey I would ever face.

As the pandemic began to escalate, we adapted to our strange new normal. Katie is a nurse practitioner and her role in healthcare helped me fully understand the severity of things, and our family began taking all the recommended precautions and locking things down tight. We masked up, worked from home, and limited our social interactions. Fortunately, my career allowed for a relatively seamless transition to working from home, enabling me to minimize the risks of COVID-19 while still meeting my professional commitments.

Professionally, I was one of the lucky ones as it related to the pandemic. My job as an automotive sales executive allowed me to easily adjust to working from my home office full-time and to continue with business almost unhindered. But I did temporarily lose one of my favorite aspects of my work: meeting face-to-face with my customers and colleagues. I relied on my in-person interactions with my customers to be successful. That was temporarily not an option.

Outside of work, my outgoing personality meant I was happiest and most comfortable when interacting with friends and family. Losing almost all face-to-face interaction really threw an enormous wrench into my life. I often felt completely displaced and struggled to find other outlets for my extroverted nature.

But, as I've done throughout my entire life, I tried to find the positive in the situation. No longer commuting, I decided to use the two extra hours I had each day to really ramp up my workouts and start to take better care of myself.

I've always worked out, but I wasn't quite where I wanted to be physically anymore. My weight had increased to over 190 pounds on my six-foot frame. While it could have been worse, for me, this was not ideal. I decided to focus on improving my diet and doing one or two cardio workouts per day. I ran on the treadmill, rode the Peloton, and boxed. I rapidly dropped ten or fifteen pounds and began feeling much better about myself. I was starting to see a silver lining to quarantining. Maybe this pandemic thing wasn't all bad!

Around late March, I started to have some abdominal pain under the upper-right side of my ribcage. I thought I had just pulled a muscle during one of my workouts and didn't give it much more attention. I figured that, like most aches and pains, it would eventually heal up and I'd be fine.

But that pain didn't go away. I didn't want to go to my doctor during the height of the pandemic, as it didn't seem much of an issue when compared to all of those battling a much greater illness, so I just put up with it and kept working out, hoping it would eventually go away.

The truth is, avoiding a visit to the doctor went a little deeper than my concern for other, higher-priority patients. This pain represented much more to me than just some ache or pain from working out. It signified a major turning point in my life. I was no longer that young and very healthy guy I once was. I didn't want to face the inevitable fact that my body was now on the decline.

While the fact that we can no longer do all the same things physically as we get older may seem obvious, I hadn't yet been willing to accept or acknowledge that reality. Though I found myself rapidly approaching the age of fifty, I was still trying to work out like I was in my twenties. I was trying desperately to fight the effects of aging and was afraid the doctor would inform me that I was losing that battle, as we all eventually do.

Call it ego. Call it pride. But let's be honest, how many of you have felt that very same thing? That need and desire to cling to your youth. Losing that was a very scary thing for me. It's kind of hard to admit it, but I suppose it would qualify as a midlife crisis. I was recognizing that I was at the age where I no longer had infinite time left in my life. I was realizing that my body wasn't invincible, and yes, my overall health was likely starting to trend downward.

I had likely injured myself doing something that wouldn't have led to injury in prior years. And beyond that, I was also healing much more slowly than a younger me would have, which was delaying me from achieving my fitness goals. So, while the pandemic gave me a good reason to avoid getting my pain checked, it also allowed me to avoid facing the fact that I was no longer as young as I wanted to be.

Two and a half months after I first felt that abdominal pain, I finally broke down and scheduled an appointment to see my doctor. I was able to use telehealth, which made the appointment simple and easy. After I explained my situation and described the ongoing pain, the doctor determined it was likely an issue with my gallbladder. Apparently, this was a common problem with people my age. So much for my plans of staying young and achieving perfect health in 2020.

As a follow up to my telehealth visit, I scheduled an ultrasound, which ultimately came back inconclusive. The next step was a hepatobiliary iminodiacetic acid, or HIDA, scan, and the results from that test showed that my gallbladder was completely nonfunctional. The doctors weren't sure why, but it had just stopped working. I was going to have to have it removed.

It might seem like a big deal to some, but it didn't really worry me. As a matter of fact, I learned that a gallbladder removal is actually a fairly common and simple procedure. I was honestly quite excited to get that mostly unnecessary organ taken out and get rid of the abdominal pain I was struggling with. I was ready to have the pain behind me so I could move forward with my health goals.

I was referred to a surgeon, and we scheduled the gallbladder removal surgery for August 19, 2020. I could see the light at the end of the tunnel.

•   •   •

While waiting for my surgery, I received devastating news. Seamus, my college roommate and one of my closest friends, had passed away. It was shocking and unexpected, an absolute gut-punch to my already tender abdomen.

I had met Seamus on move-in day when I first stepped foot on campus as a scared and nervous freshman at Michigan State

University, and he quickly became like a brother to me. He was only forty-seven years old when he died. He had two incredible kids and an amazing wife. He left us all far too soon. And while I was in the middle of facing my fears of my own mortality, his passing was a deeply painful reminder that we weren't getting any younger.

The news had pulled me into a very dark space. I needed an outlet for what was inside, so I decided to go for a run. At that time, a typical run for me was in the range of two to five miles. I hadn't run more than five miles at one time since high school, but I needed to go. I needed to focus on the simple act of placing one foot in front of the other for as long as my body needed, to pull myself out of the dark headspace that the loss of my dear friend had placed me in.

While on my run, I decided that I would run 10k as a tribute to Seamus. It was kind of an ironic tribute, as running was something he never did. But it's what I needed to do. For me. For Seamus. That day I kept on running. I ran for the emotional release. I ran to release the overwhelming sadness that was filling my heart. While I was out running on those isolated backroads, an image of Seamus popped into my head. He was in heaven, looking down and laughing at me. He was laughing because he, too, found it funny that I chose running as a way to honor him. As I pictured his smiling face, I couldn't help but smile through my tears.

I was flooded with amazing memories of all our crazy times together in college. I recalled the first time we awkwardly met on that first day. I thought about all the parties we held together at our college house on River Street, our long drives to Florida for spring break, and all the laughs along the way. I reminisced about the joy we all had at his wedding. Mostly, I just remembered the great friendship we had shared for so many years.

The death of such a close friend at such a young age was too much for me to handle, but at least running gave me a way to deal with that pain. The loss, and that amazing run, made the abdominal pain seem like less of a big deal for a brief period. I didn't know it at the time, but I had found a tool in running I could use to help me cope when life dropped me into a really grim and challenging place.

We held a memorial for Seamus near the end of July, at a park because COVID kept the funeral homes closed. Many of our college friends attended, and it was a fitting tribute to the great man we all treasured. Family and friends were always a top priority for Seamus. There's nothing he enjoyed more than sharing laughs with the people he loved. On that beautiful summer day, his family and friends shared stories, laughing, and honoring the man we had so sadly lost. It was also the point that our other three roommates and I grew even closer. While Seamus was no longer here on the planet with us, his spirit was. He brought Joel, Clayton, Matt, and me back together, tighter than ever.

• • •

As my gallbladder removal surgery approached, my upper abdominal pain continued. And now I had the added displeasure of severe back pain. The pain had gotten to the point that I was barely sleeping, and I took multiple hot baths per day to try to keep the pain under control. I was popping ibuprofen like candy.

The pain was different than anything I'd ever experienced. My inability to sleep was new too. I was struggling, but also trying to maintain my positivity. I convinced myself that this was only a short-term issue. I reasoned that all the pain was likely due to my failed gallbladder. I just needed to get to the other side of that surgery date and all would be fine.

A laparoscopic cholecystectomy, the technical term for a gallbladder removal, is a low-risk, minimally invasive outpatient procedure. The surgeon inserts a tiny video camera and some special tools through a few very small incisions in the abdomen. He then detaches and removes the gallbladder. The entire process is completed within a few hours.

On August 19, the surgery was successful. I went home that same day, just as expected. The surgeon said I'd experience a few days of postsurgical discomfort, and then have a full recovery. That's just what I'd wanted to hear. It's exactly what I had been telling myself. I could again see the light at the end of the tunnel. The abdominal and back pain were almost behind me, and I expected my life to get back to normal quickly.

But my recovery didn't go as planned. One week after the surgery, I still had horrible back pain, and now I also had severe nausea. I was getting frustrated.

In hindsight, I was not being as honest as I should have been with my surgeon. In my postsurgery consultation, I felt worse than I indicated. I barely mentioned the back pain and nausea and chose to focus only on ways I was improving. I had no baseline for how I should feel, so I chose the positive outlook and assumed I was recovering normally.

It was probably another example of my unwillingness to accept my health being anything less than what I wanted it to be. It wasn't that I was trying to be tough in front of the surgeon; I was trying to will myself back to full health. I kept waiting for things to get better.

They got worse.

CHAPTER 4

THE WORST NEWS POSSIBLE

"Um, you're yellow, Dusty," Katie said matter-of-factly.

It was September 9, and I had woken up in really bad shape. The back pain was worse than ever, I was extremely nauseated, and I had barely slept in weeks. I was three weeks postsurgery, and my health continued its downward slide.

My nonmedical mind couldn't quite figure out what the hell "you're yellow" meant, and Katie's calm medical-professional delivery of this seemingly scary news wasn't putting my mind at ease. Katie carefully explained to me that I had jaundice and needed to get to the hospital right away.

She rushed me to our local hospital, where I had a CT scan. The emergency room doctors felt additional testing was likely needed, which was more than their little hospital could handle, so I was loaded into an ambulance and transported to a larger hospital about twenty miles away. After I arrived, I spent a few uncomfortable and anxiety-riddled hours in the emergency room without Katie, who couldn't come in because of COVID restrictions.

Those first few hours in the ER were especially difficult. The hospital was already at capacity upon my arrival, so they wheeled me over to an empty corner and left me there on my own. It was dark and depressing in there. I was scared and in severe pain. My phone had died, so I had nothing to distract me from the spiraling thoughts of what could be wrong with me. And without Katie, I felt lost.

I was extremely lucky to be married to a healthcare expert, and I typically leaned hard on Katie regarding any and all medical topics. But on that day, I didn't have that option. She couldn't be there with me. So there I was, alone and scared in that dark corner of the emergency room, with my yellow skin signaling that there was something seriously wrong happening inside of me.

I was starting to panic. Sweat was beading on my forehead. I was so restless. What in the hell was wrong with me? I mean, I was yellow. I was lying there all alone, with seemingly no one doing anything to help. I started to become extremely frustrated.

I logically understood the situation: too many sick people, not enough caretakers. But in the moment, logic was thrown out the window. My frustration also went deeper than the aggravation with my momentary lack of care. I was also pissed off at the bigger picture: My recovery wasn't going as I had planned or hoped, and I couldn't do anything about it.

I was supposed to be fully recovered by now and back to my normal life, minus one nonfunctioning gallbladder. But I wasn't even close to being fully recovered; I was getting worse. I was in extreme pain and trapped alone in a dark ER corner with no support system. Why me? All I kept thinking was that I should've completed my simple surgery and be moving on with my life right now. I should be focusing on my family, my career, my health, and my workouts.

For months, my single-minded focus had been only on a return to "normal" health. That strong desire for a return to the status quo led me to minimize the severity of what I was experiencing. I'd been lying to myself. Hiding from how sick I had become. Trying to convince myself I was on a quick path to recovery and a return to my healthy status.

Unfortunately, that was all far away from the path I was on. The emergency room staff ended up admitting me. I was given a load of pain meds, scheduled for more scans, and left alone in a hospital room with my mind racing with fears of what might come next.

I was yellow because my liver was leaking bile into my abdomen. The doctors' assumption was that the surgeon may have nicked something during my gallbladder surgery, which led to a leak. I would have to undergo more scans to find the leak, and then a surgeon would go back in to see if they could seal it up.

I spent that entire next week in the hospital. On my second and third days there, I went through more scans, including another HIDA, a CT, and multiple MRIs. While my memory of that week is hazy, I vividly remember those scans. Having an irregular skin tone and knowing your liver is inexplicably leaking fluid is stressful enough, but the added anxiety of what might show up on those scans was far worse.

The most unpleasant scans were the MRIs. The entire MRI process became a complete physical and mental challenge. After the technician hooked an IV into my arm, they slowly loaded me into a long tube that is roughly the size of a coffin. I'm not claustrophobic, but the tight fit is far from comfortable, and the opposite of a calming experience.

After being loaded in, I was guided through a variety of prompts to hold my breath as the machine loudly banged and whirred around my head. My back still hurt badly, so I strained to hold the air still in my lungs while lying on top of the hard slab of the MRI table. I remember struggling, on the verge of hyperventilating.

Beyond the physical discomfort, I was fighting the fears that were creeping in and filling my head with the worst of what might be wrong. I had a lot of time to think while stuck in that tube. I was close to a mental breakdown. The combination of the confined space, the extreme pain I was experiencing, the near hyperventilation, and the fears filling my brain was a recipe that threw me into complete disarray.

I had to get a grip on things, so I willfully and forcefully pushed positive thoughts into my head. "Everything is going to be all right. Have faith," I told myself over and over. "Stay positive. Mind over matter." I started to have some deep dialogue with God. I began to pray while focusing on my breathing, trying to be in control of it.

The combination of repeated positive mantras and continuous prayer finally helped me calm down a bit, and I found I was regaining some sense of control of the situation—at least the catastrophizing going on in my mind, which made it a bit more tolerable. The rest of the series of scans were equally difficult, but I deployed my new strategy of concentrated positive thoughts, prayers, and focused breathing and got through them.

My doctors ultimately found my liver leak. They immediately scheduled me for surgery to repair it and put in a stent to stop the bile from leaking further. But they were still unable to conclusively determine why it was leaking in the first place. Regardless, they were able to fix me, and I was about to regain my natural color.

When the doctors and radiologists at the hospital were reviewing the scans, they found something they weren't looking for: There appeared to be a mass of some sort in the head of my pancreas. As they were giving me the details, and they said the word "mass," my heart stopped beating. I was frozen in a state of disbelief and fear.

A mass? Seriously? This wasn't what I signed up for. The plan was only for a simple gallbladder removal and then a return to normal. Now I had some kind of mass in my pancreas? Why me? I was starting to freak out again.

My doctors, on the other hand, didn't seem overly concerned about it. Apparently, I was not the demographic for pancreatic cancer. They told me that it was likely just a mass of fluid caused by the gallbladder and subsequent liver issues I experienced. They repeatedly reassured me that it was likely nothing to be worried about but also strongly advised that once I was out of the hospital I meet with an oncologist and schedule a biopsy, just to be safe.

The idea of meeting with an oncologist was anything but reassuring to me. But I believe everything in life happens for a reason. People don't just enter our lives by happenstance; God puts them in our lives when we need them most. While I was in the hospital, there happened to be an oncologist from one of the local affiliated cancer institutes doing rounds. My team had Dr. A stop in to see me for a consultation.

My first impression of her was very positive. She had a bedside manner that immediately put me at ease. "At ease" was not a feeling that I had experienced much in the hospital leading up to that meeting. Dr. A was able to help me fully understand the biopsy process I would be going through once out of the hospital, as well as all the potential outcomes, from the not-so-serious to the worst possible.

Dr. A was obviously an expert in her field, but that wasn't what stuck with me after meeting her. Her calming presence made any potential outcome, even a bad one, seem like something that we would be able to manage if those were the cards I was dealt. I decided that using her cancer institute to do the biopsy would be the easiest and best choice. Even though I was telling myself it was just a formality, deep in my heart I knew that it was important to have Dr. A involved in my care, despite having just met her.

With my leak fixed and a revised plan in place, they sent me home, and I took the last few weeks of September to recover. At the end of the month, Katie and I made the one-hour drive south to downtown Detroit, where I met with the biopsy surgeon for my initial consultation. It was supposed to be a quick visit, knowing I would return at a later date for the actual biopsy.

Looking back, I think it was at this point when the phrase "expect the unexpected" became the headline of my life.

When the biopsy team joined us in the exam room, things quickly took one of those unexpected turns. I was still very weak following my hospital stay. I had been struggling to eat and drink enough water and had lost a lot of weight and strength. Based on my sickly condition, combined with the results of my pre-consultation bloodwork that the biopsy team ran, they quickly decided that I needed to be admitted to the hospital and scheduled for an urgent biopsy the following day.

I hope my biopsy surgeon doesn't play poker. I vividly remember the look that passed across his face when he reviewed my bloodwork before deciding to admit me. He projected "Uh-oh, this isn't good" without saying a single word. At the time, I was still trying to bluff myself, refusing to acknowledge the severity of what I was facing. So my mind quickly pushed that telling look of his aside, allowing me to avoid any thought of potential cancer.

So, there I was again, alone in a hospital without my healthcare advocate by my side. In less than a month we had gone from "Um, you're yellow!" to "Wow. Could I really have cancer?"

•   •   •

I tried the best I could to settle in for a long night of minimal sleep as I anxiously awaited my biopsy. It was almost impossible to get comfortable and rest. The overly white, overly sterile feel of my hospital room was far from settling. The bed was also extremely firm, which didn't help my ongoing back pain. On top of all that, I was completely alone, and my head was spinning with troublesome thoughts. I spent the night tossing and turning, restlessly awaiting the morning.

I found myself starting to spiral, and I really started to worry. It was the first time the C word started to seriously creep into my mind. I kept talking myself out of the many different possibilities. I told myself there was no way I could really have cancer. I was too young. I was too healthy. I had no family history that put me at risk. I told myself it was just a simple fluid mass caused by the gallbladder surgery and subsequent complications. That was a much more plausible explanation. That was my preferred diagnosis, the one I would cling to for as long as I possibly could.

But somewhere in my subconscious, I knew my life was about to change. I had recognized that knowing look during my bloodwork review, that recognition that only an experienced surgeon who has been through this thousands of times already knows. He knew. I knew he knew. And yet I was in complete denial about the fact that I might have cancer.

I was doing all sorts of mental gymnastics to reason with what was playing out right before me. And I was doing it alone. Having no support system by my side made my growing fears and concerns even more of a challenge to deal with, as all the worst-case scenarios kept playing out in my head. I needed and wanted Katie by my side so badly, to lean on her for support. She could have helped distract me from myself. It would have been so beneficial to have her there to push that enormous elephant out of the room. I still wonder about all those other patients in similar situations who were forced to be alone with their illnesses during COVID restrictions, not knowing what would happen from one minute to the next.

I don't know how I made it through that night, but the next day I eventually went in for the biopsy. Katie returned to the hospital that morning, sitting nervously in the waiting room to hear the results.

The next few hours were pivotal, and we both knew going in the outcome would potentially be life-changing. Regardless, both of us—me lying on that bed in pre-op and her sitting anxiously in the waiting room—chose to hold on to our hopes that the biopsy would show that mass inside me was nonthreatening.

I will never forget what happened when I woke up from that surgery.

I was alone, still extremely groggy from anesthesia, and lying in an uncomfortable hospital bed in the post-op area. The room was dark and empty, although I could hear some nurses not too far away in an adjacent room. OK, that's finally over. Now the doctor can come in and tell me there was no sign of cancer, and I can go home and finally begin my recovery.

The doctor did come in, but that wasn't the message he had for me.

. . .

I am a people person, an extreme extrovert. My wife and kids will tell you that I talk to everyone, all the time. I'm sure it can be kind of annoying, but they know I genuinely care about meeting new people and learning their life stories. I'm someone who puts a huge value on relationships, and I'm also someone who's pretty good at reading the room and judging character.

The read I had on my biopsy surgeon, from the very first moment of meeting him, was that he was obviously an expert in his field and an excellent surgeon. But from our initial conversation, I knew he was not going to be someone I enjoyed interacting with. Knowing this was just a biopsy, I knew I wouldn't have to have an ongoing relationship with him. All I needed was for him to carefully go in through my throat and abdomen and cut out a small sample of that mass to be evaluated by the pathologist. And that's precisely what he had done.

But when he came into that recovery room to talk to me, as I lay there, trying to shake off the last foggy clouds of anesthesia, his poor bedside manner became a bigger issue.

The room was still dark when he mysteriously appeared out of nowhere and was standing directly above me. The moment we made eye contact, he quickly blurted out "Mr. Mysen, I'm sorry to have to tell you this, but you have pancreatic cancer. In my expert opinion it is non-operable. There's not much that can be done. I'm sorry to be the one who must tell you this news." Then he left, as quickly as he had appeared.

It felt like a drive-by diagnosis.

He had hit me with the most devastating news possible, then just walked away. He left me lying there all alone, trying to process what I'd just heard. This was the most horrible news I had ever received in my life, and it was given hit-and-run style. As cliché as it sounds, my life truly did pass before my eyes in that instant. Everything I loved in life felt like it was about to be lost. My life was about to be over.

I couldn't breathe. I had pancreatic cancer.

•   •   •

After hearing the diagnosis, my mind was suddenly flooded with thoughts and images of my soon-to-be-widowed wife and my four amazing kids who were about to lose their father long before they should. The tears came hard and fast as I was glued to the hospital bed, alone and crying my eyes out.

In retrospect, all my health issues in 2020 now made complete sense. My gallbladder didn't just randomly stop working or fail because I was getting old. It stopped functioning because there was a big ol' tumor in my pancreas, blocking the flow of things. Like so many things in life, our health symptoms have a way of putting us on a crazy hunt looking for, and eventually finding out, what's really going on inside our bodies. Many times, like in my case, what we find is unfortunately not what we were hoping for.

Mine was a kind of cancer that carried one of the worst mortality rates across all the cancers. According to the American Cancer Society, the five-year survival rate for pancreatic cancer is only 12 percent. More than half of pancreatic cancer patients die within just three months of diagnosis. I had just received a diagnosis of a type of cancer that takes 88 percent of its patients within just a few years and over half of them in less than three months. There's no good way to learn you have cancer, but this was definitely not the way you want to find out.

Unfortunately, my wife had a similar experience. Katie had been sitting in that waiting area for much longer than she had expected. To be fair, my surgery was delayed for a few hours, but while I was lying in pre-op, waiting for my turn, no one had bothered to tell her my surgery was being pushed back. By the time she received the call that I was in post-op recovery, it must have felt like she'd been waiting for days. As a nurse practitioner, she knew that things had taken way longer than planned and that the news she was about to receive was likely not going to be good.

She was making her way to see me, traveling from the first floor waiting area down to the basement post-op recovery room. As she started to exit the elevator and head in to find me, she bumped into the surgeon. It seems impossible that he could become less empathetic, but when he saw Katie, he burst out: "Mrs. Mysen, I'm sorry, but your husband has inoperable pancreatic cancer. He's over there." He awkwardly pointed in the direction of the post-op room.

After Katie was able to collect herself, she finally joined me. Our reunion was bittersweet and filled with crying, holding each other, and crying some more. We really couldn't speak of the cancer at that point. There were no words that could articulate the full trauma of what we had just gone through. My life, and the life of my family, would never be the same.

CHAPTER 5

THE BEARER OF BAD NEWS

Lying in that dark recovery room, the night of the drive-by cancer diagnosis, I felt like I had reached the end of the road. All seemed lost. I was knocked down. I was close to knocked out. But I chose to get up and fight. That was the beginning of my battle and my new life as a cancer warrior.

It was like cancer flipped and completely rewrote my personal script. My life story changed so fast I got whiplash. Getting old was suddenly no longer a concern. Growing old became a goal; one that now seemed completely unachievable. Being able to live past the age of forty-nine simply became a hope and a prayer.

I was just told my life would end, probably suddenly, and that I only had months, a few years if I was lucky, to live. I felt like life was playing a cruel joke on me. I had been so focused on staying young, and now I was suddenly being told that cancer was going to take away any chance of actually growing old.

The irony wasn't lost on me. My concerns and perspective had shifted almost 180 degrees. My previous worries now became my one and only hope. My motivation had suddenly changed drastically, and now I was worried only about whether I would make it to the age of fifty.

My crazy health journey had taken me on a roller coaster of a ride. I began the year überfocused on my health: a year that I was going to work myself back to the condition of a much younger version of myself. It then transitioned to months of frustrations with my health, what I thought were just the realities of aging. Ultimately ending with a diagnosis of a horrific cancer that absolutely no one saw coming.

I had received the most devastating news of my life, and I had no idea what I was about to endure or how long I'd be able to hang on. But, when we get knocked down hard, we face our toughest and most important decisions. Was this diagnosis going to keep me down, or would I get back up and fight?

• • •

After that biopsy in September 2020, I was still so weak and dehydrated that they kept me for one additional night. I was emotionally destroyed and still trying to process the devastating news. The last thing I wanted was to spend one more night alone in a hospital room away from my family, but I didn't have a choice.

I had cancer, but I think Katie was worse off on that day. During our eighteen-plus years, we had handled all the big things together, as a team. But this one, the biggest one, she had to do without me. She had to make the hour drive home alone, her head filled with fears and doubts, and then be the one to tell our four children that their dad had cancer. The fact that she had to handle that burden alone floods my heart with guilt to this day.

She told each of them individually. Tristen, who was twenty-one and away at college, learned first over FaceTime. He tried to handle it like an adult. As a pre-med student, he went the logical route, trying to understand the situation from a medical viewpoint and figure out what the next steps were for me. But as a young adult who was learning all the gory details about horrible diseases like mine, he understood pretty quickly how bad of a diagnosis I had received. The fact that he was a five-hour drive away from us didn't make it any easier.

After Katie told Landon, he went straight to his room to digest the news. He needs to be alone to think. This is why I always worry most about him in difficult situations. It's almost impossible to get a read on how he's truly handling things. But it's his way, and Katie and I have always tried to honor and respect that.

Our daughter Parker wears her heart on her sleeve and is much more open with her emotions and feelings. She's an empath, so when someone else is hurting, she truly feels that hurt herself. She started crying and worrying for me the moment Katie told her. She was able to openly express all her concerns to Katie right after learning of the diagnosis. Just picturing her reaction to the news brings tears to my eyes.

Grady, our youngest, is super inquisitive. He was just eight years old at the time, which meant he didn't fully understand the severity of the diagnosis, but he understood enough to know I was very sick, and it wasn't good. But he immediately jumped to the outcome, the "how do they fix Dad?" part. This was probably because he loved watching medical shows on TV. *The Good Doctor* was one of his favorites. He peppered Katie with a million questions. He asked about everything from the details of how my pancreas worked to what types of treatments I'd be receiving. He was eternally optimistic about everything and certain I'd be fully cured quickly. But his inquisitive nature meant he had to ask all the questions to learn how it could be fixed, and how quickly—all of which were very tough questions for Katie to try to answer to an eight-year-old.

Although each kid dealt with the awful news in their own unique way, for Katie, telling each was exactly the same: It broke her heart each time.

CHAPTER 6

SO I HAVE CANCER. NOW WHAT?

There's a reason most people don't like hanging out in hospitals: They suck. They all have that sterile, unpleasant, sad feeling to them. But as I tried to focus on my environment and take my mind off my uncertain future, I noticed mine seemed overly white, and the temperature was just a little too cold. The air felt stale, and it was eerily quiet. It was the absolute last place in the world I wanted to be during that critical moment in my life.

I lay staring at the white-tiled ceiling, tears in my eyes, trying to figure it all out. The situation took me to a very somber place. I was overwhelmed with very deep, very dark, very intense images of my own funeral: my widowed wife, my fatherless children, and my friends and family, all mourning my life. The end of me was vividly projected center stage in my mind as I lay in my own sorrow.

There was no one to converse with, to distract me, to pull me out of those dark thoughts. No doctors, no nurses, no shared hospital roommate. Just me, sitting with my own morbid diagnosis, with those dark, scary thoughts. I was completely stuck in them, and they were sucking me down into a very bad place. I had to get out of there but was trapped in my own head.

After endless hours of crying and processing the news, I realized I would have to dig deep down to find a way to pull myself together. If I didn't, I knew, somehow, things could get worse. I had to do something to change my focus. I needed to shift my thoughts to something more positive. I needed to bring myself back.

I wasn't religious growing up and didn't really go to church. I had begun to attend church more regularly with Katie and the kids a few years prior but I was still very early in my church experience. But having a life-threatening diagnosis has a way of slamming a person quickly and firmly into their faith. And that's what helped me to shift my focus and start to pull myself out of the darkness that cancer had pushed me into.

I was never a guy who could recite a lot from the Bible, but for some reason late that night, one of my favorite pieces of scripture popped powerfully into my head: Proverbs 3: 5,6. "Trust in the Lord with all your heart, and lean not on your own understanding. In all your ways submit to Him, and He will make your path straight."

I began repeating it over and over and over again in my head. Eventually, slowly, I found that I started to feel a bit calmer. Those simple words started to lift my spirits and allowed me to see just a little bit of light. I realized very clearly that maybe I wasn't meant to understand why this was happening to me; maybe I just needed to trust that it was part of God's plan for me. I needed to hand it all over to Him, and He would somehow help get me through it.

After rounds of repeating that scripture, my mind shifted directions slightly and a mantra popped into my head: "FAITH over fear."

It's a miracle, really, that when we're forced to look death directly in the eyes, these simple uplifting thoughts, these mantras and sayings, can come to us like a little gift. I didn't know it yet that night, but that little mantra would become the headline of my personal playbook, my cancer-fighting plan, and the words I would fall back on for everything I would face in life going forward. "*Faith* over fear." Again, "*Faith* over fear." And again, and again, and again. It was divine. That mantra literally pushed the fear, which was making a bad situation so much worse, right out of my mind and body. Those simple words offered me faith and hope. It was a miracle.

In the middle of that fateful night, in that cold and unsettling hospital room, I was able to gain some sense of control over my fears and emotions. I was even able to get a little sleep. Those words continued to carry me long after that first night. I have repeated them in my head thousands of times over the course of my battle with cancer, and every time they've helped to give me some peace.

• • •

The miracles were not over for me in those first twenty-four hours as a cancer warrior. In the middle of the night, an angel of a nurse on the overnight shift came in to check on me.

Out of nowhere she bluntly asked, "Mr. Mysen, are you a Christian?" I think she'd noticed the cross I always wear around my neck. But the question caught me off guard.

After collecting myself briefly, I answered that, yes, I was a Christian.

I will never in my life forget what happened next. She asked if she could pray over me. Again, I was a little caught off guard by the question, but in my heart, it suddenly felt like that was exactly what I needed. So I told her she could.

As she put her hand on my chest and started praying, I felt strength and hope for the first time in days, weeks, even months. I don't remember everything she prayed in detail, but she continued for what felt like a half hour or more. I vividly remember her reciting Isaiah 53:5. "By his stripes we are healed." She repeated it multiple times and told me that by Jesus's stripes (wounds), I would be healed of my cancer. At that time, I knew enough about pancreatic cancer statistics to know that me being healed of my cancer was improbable. But when she prayed, I felt something shift inside me. I somehow knew what she said was true. More importantly, I believed it. I felt it deep in my heart.

·   ·   ·

When Katie arrived the next day, we were able to meet with a few of the doctors from the oncology team. Their view of my situation seemed slightly better than the biopsy surgeon's. While it wasn't great news, it was better than we had originally thought based on the initial crude delivery.

This fresh set of doctors generally agreed with the biopsy surgeon that my tumor might not be removable via surgery, staging it as borderline resectable, which means that they weren't confident they could surgically remove it, but also that the surgical option wasn't completely ruled out either. There was still a possibility that at some point in the future, we might be able to try what's called a Whipple procedure, which is the only hope for any form of a cure for pancreatic cancer.

A Whipple procedure is a high-risk, complicated surgery that removes the head of the pancreas, including the unwanted tumor, along with the first part of the small intestine (duodenum), and the bile duct. Pancreatic cancer is very aggressive. Without this procedure to remove the tumor, it's almost impossible to stop the cancer from growing and spreading. The Whipple procedure is the only treatment that gives any chance for prolonged survival. It is the only real chance a person with pancreatic cancer has.

But at that time the tumor was too close to one of my main arteries. This meant the probability of damaging that artery during surgery was way too high. One small nick of that artery would typically lead to the patient bleeding out and dying. The odds weren't really in my favor, so they opted for chemotherapy treatments in the hopes that the tumor would shrink, allowing for some separation from my superior mesenteric artery, that critical artery that fed blood to my pancreas and small and large intestines. If the chemo could create some margin between the tumor and the artery, it could allow the team to resect the tumor without such a high surgical risk.

This diagnosis wasn't ideal, but I took it as a positive, as a new lifeline toward hope. And let's be very clear: It was far, far better than the gruff assessment from the night before, which implied that I should just accept the bad news and prepare to die. What a difference a day can make. After twenty-four hours of fear and uncertainty, I was now propped up with a little hope and released from the hospital. All I wanted to do was hug my kids tight and start drawing up new plans for this battle against my cancer.

CHAPTER 7

FAITH OVER FEAR

I realized right away that I was going to need to lean strongly into my faith.

I view faith as simply having a trust in something bigger than yourself. For me, putting that in action meant being a Christian, believing and trusting in God and his son Jesus Christ. Hebrews 11:1 says, "Now faith is the assurance of things hoped for, the conviction of things not seen." I have never seen Jesus appear before me, but I have 100 percent faith and confidence that He exists. He's watched over me and guided my journey through life, specifically during my battle with cancer.

For you, faith may be a belief and trust in another God based on your religious preference. Or maybe you're not religious but you hold faith in something else larger than yourself, like having faith in modern medicine. Whatever your beliefs are, or whatever spiritual path you're on, I honor that. I'm not here to tell you what to have faith in. My point here is only that across all practices, the simple act of keeping faith is a way to keep yourself connected to something bigger, something that can hold you up. Especially when we face our biggest struggles in life, like fighting a terminal illness such as cancer.

My parents raised our family as Christians, but we didn't study the Bible or regularly attend Sunday service. Our spirituality came from the clear values they taught us, which were consistently held up in our household. On the rare occasion I did go to church, I felt like I didn't learn enough to feel like I belonged.

Three or four years prior to my diagnosis, Katie and I decided that we wanted our kids to be exposed to church more regularly. Katie had attended church as a child and was missing the sense of community. We had tried attending other churches together before, but never found a great fit and had never gone consistently.

Katie and I eventually found a local nondenominational church that seemed to be a perfect fit. The church services were very practical, not going too deep into theology or too far over my head. The messages the pastoral team shared in each sermon opened my eyes to new and interesting perspectives and became a guiding light to my daily actions every week. To top it off, listening to the music from the church band was like getting to watch a high-level concert every Sunday. They also had a large, very diverse, and extremely friendly group of parishioners.

Until that point I had always felt out of place and awkward with religion. I think it was a mix of my insecurities about fitting in without having the religious upbringing to lean back on, along with feeling unaccepted as the "new guy" by those lifelong churchgoers. At our new church I never felt that way. The community welcomed me and my family in, and it was exactly what I needed to allow myself to open my heart. I was able to listen to and, more importantly, receive the messages fully. I learned about Christ and his lessons in a supportive environment alongside my family. Each week I was learning more from the Bible and the incredible life lessons it provided. I finally felt like I belonged, and I was able to connect with the teachings in a way that allowed me to implement those lessons into my life.

My cancer diagnosis took my walk with Christ and rapidly turned it into an all-out run. Cancer is just too big of a monster to face on your own; I needed more strength than I had in my body and mind. Without my faith, there's no way that I would have been able to face and overcome my fears. I truly believe I wouldn't have made it much past my initial diagnosis.

I'm not saying people are meant to get cancer—that sounds horrible. But I do believe that God puts us on our path for a reason. I believe He gives us the experiences that will help us find our way on that path, no matter how difficult they may be. Those experiences are the mountains we must climb, the codes we must crack. The first test of any challenge is how we accept what He gives us, and the second test is whether we're able to trust the path He is guiding us on.

Fighting cancer got much easier when I chose to see my situation as just being God's plan. It makes no sense to me why some people get cancer while most others do not. Why do some survive their cancer battles, while others die way too soon? It's inexplicable. That's why I prefer to think of it as just God's plan, which, per Proverbs 3:5–6, we are not meant to understand. He has a plan for all of us, even if the path He has put us on seems incomprehensible.

For some of us, that plan includes getting cancer. For most others, it thankfully does not. Some of those cancer warriors will live through that battle, and others will sadly not survive. But all those outcomes are simply a part of God's plan. My faith has led me to do my best to accept that plan.

•　　•　　•

I'd always avoided discussing the Bible or scripture, mostly because I was relatively ignorant on the topic and was extremely fearful of exposing that ignorance. I had this unsubstantiated but strong belief that devout religious people were somehow elitist and would be unaccepting of me. And I felt my upbringing had set me too far behind to ever fit in.

In hindsight, that seems to go completely against what I now see as the core of Christianity, but it was how I had always felt, so I avoided religious discussions as much as possible. Even as I started to feel more comfortable in our new church and was learning at a rapid pace, I still largely avoided discussions on religion due to my ingrained fear of sounding ignorant and not fitting in.

But as I started my cancer treatments shortly after diagnosis, I started to dive even deeper into the Bible. As I did, I started to push through my fears and began posting on Facebook scripture that touched me. I started to make my faith a part of the public story of my fight with cancer. My faith had been carrying me through my fight in private, in my mind and in my heart, and now I was taking it public.

I also began adding "#FaithOverFear" to the end of every one of those Facebook posts. It was the phrase that had already helped carry me through as I tried to fight my fears, but it now became my public mantra that I shared almost daily with my friends and family. In response to my posts, people would share additional verses from the Bible that they thought would help me. People also started sharing many worship songs to help inspire me and lift me up.

My faith grew stronger the more I shared it with others. It became part of a beautiful circle that helped me grow and gave me so much extra strength for my fight. The expression of my faith in Jesus in a public space brought so many additional people into my life and into my support system. I suddenly had an army of prayer warriors praying for my healing and supporting me in every way possible. I received countless cards and letters with kind words, prayers, and scripture in them. Some even sent small spiritual gifts, like the "Full Armor of God" coin I received with the words of Ephesians 6:10–18 engraved on it. I carried that coin with me through almost the entirety of my battle.

I suddenly had other cancer warriors reaching out to me as well, praying for me and receiving my prayers in return. When I apprehensively shared that first piece of scripture on Facebook, I had no idea the ripple effect it would have in helping me, as well as many others in similar dire situations. I had avoided expressing my faith publicly due to an irrational fear of being judged. Once I finally pushed past that fear, I was able to see the true power that faith can have.

. . .

As a child, Katie annually attended a small church camp along the shores of Lake Huron in Michigan. Our children followed suit, attending that same camp once they were old enough. In the middle of my cancer battle, while our boys were there at the basketball camp, Katie volunteered as the camp nurse and stayed for the week, enjoying the camp experience and taking care of all the various ankle sprains and other minor injuries the campers incurred.

Parker and I decided to make the one-hour drive to visit Katie and the boys for a day. We spent the afternoon following Katie, watching the campers, including our boys, play many games of basketball. After we joined them for dinner, I was pleasantly surprised when the camp dean asked if Katie and I would join the camp counselors for their nightly prayer meeting. While the campers were younger, the counselors were mostly college-age volunteers who had chosen to give back to the camp they had once attended. Tristen, who was playing college basketball at the time and was home for the summer, was a counselor that year.

After dinner, while our younger kids and the other campers prepared for the evening activities, Katie and I joined the counselors at their prayer meeting in the chapel. After giving a brief introduction of who I was and what I was battling, the dean asked me if it would be all right if he and the counselors prayed over me.

To be honest, it made me a little uncomfortable. Being the center of attention simply for being in a bad situation was a little unnerving. I still wasn't comfortable with being someone who needed help. It was also a new religious situation for me, as I had never seen anyone prayed over by a group like this. Finally, it was a new experience that included complete strangers, as I only knew one of the counselors, my son Tristen. But even though it felt a little awkward, it also felt instinctively like something I needed and should do. I thanked the dean and told him that they could indeed pray over me.

There were approximately twenty counselors, all young adults. They surrounded me, laid their collective hands on me, and began to pray together, over me, for me. The intimidation I initially felt was quickly replaced with feelings of joy and strength. As they were praying over me, I could feel my faith growing. I felt almost weightless, as if their prayers were somehow lifting me off the ground. These amazing young people, who didn't know me at all, prayed and shared their love in unison. It was powerful! My faith had never felt so strong.

These incredible young people all prayed that I would overcome my cancer. And while I knew the poor odds of overcoming pancreatic cancer, their prayers were so powerful that I immediately believed I *would* overcome it. Their energy and focus gave me even more hope and strength. They grew my faith that evening.

The power of prayer and of faith can be a pretty amazing thing if we can just get out of our own way and simply allow ourselves to receive.

•   •   •

I once read a devotional centered around Psalm 23:4 and Matthew 14:22–33 that really stuck with me and spoke to me. Psalm 23:4 says, "Even though I walk through the darkest valley, I will fear no evil, for You are with me; Your rod and Your staff, they comfort me."

The devotional talked about how we've all faced struggles, but those of us who are fighters are somehow always able to get through those struggles. We never quit. We can listen to and follow that little voice in our head that says, "Just keep going." That voice is God! He is always with you, even in the darkest valley. He is there to comfort you, to ease your fears, to help you move forward.

Matthew 14:22–33 tells the story in which Jesus sends his disciples out on a boat on the Sea of Galilee in the middle of the night during an enormous storm. They were in a terrifying situation—a terror that I could easily relate to as I battled my cancer. Jesus put the disciples in that situation to teach them that following Him did not mean that life would be easy. They would still have to face the difficult storms. But by following Jesus, they could rely on a strength that was far greater than their own when those storms hit. With Jesus, they did not need to fear the storm. As Jesus came into the boat, the storms completely stopped.

We cannot overcome the storms of life on our own; we need something bigger to handle them.

I frequently referenced that story during my cancer battle, and it reminded me that the storm of cancer was far too big for me alone. I needed Jesus in my boat. I was in a dark valley, but I didn't need to worry because I had Him with me. He would lead me out of the valley, out of the storm. I realized I absolutely needed my faith. I needed Jesus with me at all times. I needed to trust that Jesus would guide me through the storm. That is what faith is, and it was a major factor in how I was able to stay in the fight against my pancreatic cancer.

CHAPTER 8

WE HAVE A PLAN

Katie had handled the heavy task of notifying our kids of my diagnosis, but I was the one left with the difficult undertaking of informing my parents. They lived on the other side of the state, and with COVID, there was no way to tell them in person. I'd have to tell them the horrible news over the phone.

It wasn't an easy assignment, and I had to spend a few hours giving myself a pep talk before I could dial their number. I felt guilty. How do you tell two amazing people, who had done everything in their power to give their son the best possible life, that he'd very likely die well before them?

We all know it can happen, but it's tragic when a parent is put in a position where they must contemplate the death of a child. This is not the natural order of things. That's what I struggled with the most as I prepared to dial their number and give them news that would crush their hearts.

Once I was on the phone with them, I could barely get the words out: "Mom, Dad, the news isn't good. I have pancreatic cancer. They don't think the tumor can be removed." Those few words took way longer than they should have to form and escape my mouth.

My voice was trembling, not much more than a feeble whisper. I felt like each word I spoke slowly slipped out and slapped them hard across the face. I cried a lot on that call. They did too.

But they did what amazing parents do: They supported me fully. They loved me and comforted me. And even though they were heartbroken beyond belief, they encouraged me and tried to give me a little hope. They somehow found a way to push their own pain aside and do everything in their power to try to take my pain and suffering away. That is what parents do, after all. For that, I am eternally grateful.

Mostly, they just listened to my fears. They let me vent. They showed empathy over my concerns about the future. They highlighted how loved I was, and how much support I had for the battle I was about to face. They tried to help me find my positivity and tried to give me a little hope, any hope.

I felt responsible for the pain I knew it caused them, though. I talked to them multiple times a week, even more frequently than we had before I had cancer. Every time I talked to them, I felt like I was laying this horrible situation back on their plates. I cried so often on those calls. It was not because I was sad for myself. I had accepted my situation. I had accepted my fight. I cried because it made me sad to put my parents through pain and emotional suffering. They had done everything in their power to give me an amazing life, and this is how I was repaying them?

•   •   •

I was soon able to schedule my initial appointment with Dr. A, the oncologist who had been making rounds when I had my liver leak. That first appointment in early October was rough. I was very weak and still in extreme pain. I was also very anxious to attend that first appointment and learn the details of my treatment plan. I was a physical and emotional mess.

After some bloodwork and vitals, Katie and I were given a quick tour of the facility, then we met with Dr. A and two of her infusion center nurses. I had no idea at the time how important these three amazing women were about to become in my life.

I was in particularly rough physical shape that day. I could barely keep my eyes open at the conference table as Dr. A explained the treatment process. I heard some of the details of the chemotherapy treatments I'd be undertaking, but to be honest, I could barely focus on the discussion at all. I think I was also dissociating a bit. My mind could not handle all that was being thrown at me. I was pretty much useless in that critical first meeting.

Thank God I had Katie there with me. I trusted that she would fully understand the plan being presented, and that she would be able to translate everything into less technical terms for me after the fact. Given my condition, I had no choice but to rely on her to be my ears and voice.

To me, the treatments and what I was about to go through were just what they were. I couldn't give any knowledgeable input to what the best treatment course for my diagnosis was anyway, and knew already that I trusted Dr. A, and would follow her lead regardless of what treatment plan that called for.

So, I just sat there, eyes barely open, grimacing in pain, nodding occasionally in response to the vast amount of information being poured onto me. At one point in our discussions in that conference room, I got so exhausted and was in so much pain that I asked if I could take a break and go lie in one of the recliners in the infusion center while they continued with Katie.

They were so kind and agreed to let me rest a little. One of the nurses guided me into the infusion center, set me up in a recliner, and cozied me up under a warm blanket. I fell asleep while they pieced together the details of my pending treatment plan. That would not be the last time that the amazing people on Dr. A's staff so caringly went above and beyond to help me.

On our ride home, Katie gave me the details I just hadn't been able to take in. She knew how bad I felt, so she provided a simplified version that I could easily understand. The initial plan called for five rounds of FOLFIRINOX, one of the strongest chemotherapy cocktails that can be administered. It comes with pretty harsh side effects, which include fun things like nausea, mouth and throat sores, exhaustion, loss of taste, numbness in the hands and feet, anemia, low white blood cells, and much more. Many people cannot tolerate it at all. But the hope was that because of my relatively young age (oh yeah, now I'm young again) and my relatively good health, I might be able to handle it better than most. If that turned out to be true, this was the best shot for shrinking the tumor.

My treatments would consist of seven-hour sessions in the chemo chair at the infusion center every other Monday. After each of those Mondays, I would follow up with a continued infusion, via a portable pump, that I took home for an additional forty-eight hours. On Wednesday afternoons, I would then return to the infusion center and get the pump disconnected, then have about a week-and-a-half break before starting the next round.

After those initial five rounds of the FOLFIRINOX, the plan was to do a follow-up CT scan at the end of the year, and then evaluate whether the treatments had helped shrink the tumor enough that they could attempt the Whipple procedure to resect it. Additionally, Dr. A's belief was that the chemotherapy should also help reduce some of my pain. The tumor was pressing on nerves in my back, which was the main cause of my horrible back pain. As the chemo shrunk the tumor a little, the pressure on those nerves would be reduced and the expectation was my pain would subside.

When I had first heard the words "inoperable pancreatic cancer," my blessed life came to a screeching halt. It felt like all was about to be lost, and there would be no more blessings. As we started to put together my cancer battle plan, that grim outlook started to shift slightly. I soon realized that I was in for more blessings than I could have ever imagined. It turns out that things are often not as dire as they seem on the surface, but that is never easy to see in the midst of our struggles.

CHAPTER 9

THE POWER OF POSITIVITY

I was processing the news of my cancer on multiple levels: on a spiritual level, which affected my faith; on a physical level, which affected my body; and on emotional and mental levels, which affected my heart and mind. All are strongly interconnected.

I quickly realized that my mind could rapidly send me into a downward spiral if I let it. What horrible struggles was I going to face through this journey? How bad was it really going to get? What would I have to continue to give up? What was I going to lose? What would be the legacy for my wife and kids? And on and on. I knew on that first night in that hospital bed I would need to gain some control over my mental state quickly, or it would keep going downhill fast.

Being diagnosed with cancer is obviously one of those kick-in-the-stomach moments. At first, I wanted to crawl under the blankets of that hospital bed, cry my eyes out, and just quit. Quit everything. Quit trying to figure out how to address my kids about their dad having a terminal illness. Quit trying to figure out an impossible plan for fighting an impossible disease. Quit all of it. But I didn't quit.

I eventually pulled myself together, at least a little, and decided to face the darkness that the cancer brought head-on, to dive into those painful emotions, even though I was very scared to do so. Once I was able to accept the really bad situation I was in as my reality, as the place I was in whether I wanted to be or not, I was able to start assessing how to adapt and adjust. I had cancer. Cancer sucks. That was my new reality. There was no hiding from it.

Accepting and facing that darkness was not easy at first. Once I was able to, though, I could move on to figuring out how I could best deal with it and start to move forward. For me, that started with choosing my mentality. I decided on that first night that I was going to dig deep into my soul to find every positive thing possible in that dark time. After seeing the shift within myself by repeating my mantra of "*faith* over fear," I knew that having a positive attitude was going to be critical in my battle, that it would likely have the biggest impact in aligning my body, mind, and spirit. I wasn't hiding from the darkness of my situation; I was choosing to find light, any light, to overcome the darkness in every way possible.

After making it through that first rough night in the hospital after my diagnosis, I quickly started to flip the switch from "woe is me" to forcing myself to exude positivity. And honestly, I did have to force it a little at the beginning. But I knew that my attitude was going to play a significant role in my ability to fight and deal with the adversity I was about to face. I suppose it could've gone either way. Some people see the glass half empty, and when you're delivered the kind of news that I received, I can see where it might be easier to just drain the cup. But that wasn't me. All my life I'd been a glass-half-full kind of guy, always looking to refill my cup. And not just my cup—I wanted to pour more life into other people's cups too.

So, at first, yes, I forced myself to be positive. It wasn't like, "I have cancer, let's have a party!" But "fake it until you make it" can be more than just a saying when you really need it to be. And eventually, I started to believe my own hype. I have believed in the power of positivity through my entire life, really, so why would I let cancer change that?

Cancer not only tries to destroy the physical body—it also tries to take out your emotional and mental well-being as well. I was lucky to have figured out that aspect of things on that first fateful night in the hospital. When cancer tried to pull me down, by the grace of God and with a little strength of my own, I was able to remember the most important parts of me that cancer so badly wanted to break down. I was determined to not let the cancer win easily and knew that the first line of defense against that happening was having a strong and positive mindset.

The day after I received my diagnosis of pancreatic cancer, I decided to go public and notify my wider network of friends and family on social media. I typed up a Facebook post to let them know what was going on and to ask for their prayers. I didn't want to appear sad or down from this news. I wanted to look strong. I wanted to show everyone that I planned to face this cancer head-on. I didn't want anyone feeling sorry for me. So, I rewrote that post close to ten times, until I felt it properly notified people of my new situation but also showed nothing but positivity and strength and love. I received well over 300 comments on that initial cancer post. I received more support and positivity back than I ever expected.

The positivity and strength I tried to portray in those words was responded to with so much love and positive feedback in return that it truly started to transition the positivity I was faking into my reality. It was an amazing ripple effect that completely changed how I felt about my diagnosis. The positivity I put out about what most would consider the worst news possible came back to me a hundredfold in replies.

The strength that gave me was immeasurable. It was like the virtual version of the nurse praying over me that first night in the hospital or the counselors praying over me at camp. It filled my heart with love, and it made me feel physically stronger. Reading those comments of support from so many people in my life made me believe deep in my heart that I could beat this thing. I knew after that first cancer post that I needed to continue sharing my journey with as much positivity as possible.

So those positive Facebook posts continued and became a part of my regular routine as I worked my way through my battle. I posted through every step of the way. I wrote about every scan, every twist and turn, every complication, but always in a positive manner. If I started to feel down a little, I would get a hard workout in and then post about it. The positive replies would come pouring in, helping to lift me back up. With every positive reply, I could feel my strength increasing. This process continued throughout my entire fight and became a critical coping mechanism for keeping my attitude where I needed it to be.

While I was able to transition to a positivity mindset relatively quickly, I didn't do it without first having to address the extreme negatives of my situation. Unfortunately, to truly appreciate the beautiful view from the top of the mountain, you must walk and suffer through dark valleys and climb your way out of them to get to the top. I believe that those few who have been dropped on the top and never experienced the valleys cannot truly appreciate the peaks like others. The contrast between the light of extreme happiness and positivity and the darkness of those truly emotionally gutting, kick-you-in-the-stomach bad moments in life is a good thing. We need that contrast.

Without confronting those horrible negative moments and all the emotional turmoil they produce, we can never truly get the full benefits of the positivity we can exude. I had to accept the bad as my current reality (because that's what it was), face it head-on, and slowly, step-by-step, work my way through that darkness until I could see some light. I then tried to give back a little by exuding positivity as much as possible.

There was another aspect that made staying positive so important to me. I can be a bit of a controlling person. But, for the most part, cancer takes all the control. It affects everything, down to how you feel each and every day. So, there wasn't much I could truly control in my situation, which was tough for me. But there's one thing I can most definitely always control, and that's my attitude.

Attitude is a choice. Each of us controls that. In every situation, even when burdened with the weight of having cancer, you get to choose whether you see the glass half-full or half-empty. That is a choice and something that can be controlled.

I needed at least one thing that was completely under my control. That one thing became my outlook. If I felt the darkness of negativity trying to overcome me, I made the choice to find something, anything, to immediately pick me back up. Whether it was a good workout, a nice talk with a family member or friend, or just a walk around the neighborhood; I would choose to do something. That one little thing that I could control made me feel like I was in charge of the fight. I was controlling my attitude, and cancer could not, and would not, take that away from me.

•   •   •

Before I even started my first round of chemo, I received a text message from an old high school friend. She was an occupational therapist in our hometown. She told me how inspired she was by my positive attitude. She said that in her profession she had seen so many examples of how our outlook can affect our physical struggles. Without fail, the patients she had who exhibited negativity did far worse in their recovery than those who remained positive through it all. Somehow, I had known from the very start of my cancer journey that a positive attitude would be crucial. Her stories of her patients confirmed my theory and made me push to be even more upbeat through it all.

I eventually started to see it for myself at the infusion center as I went through my chemo treatments. The other patients who always seemed to be in a bad mood and sulking seemed to get sicker. Others always seemed upbeat, with a smile on their faces. Every single one of those more positive patients seemed to be handling the effects of chemo much better. I got to know many of those more positive patients pretty well over the course of our treatments. We greeted each other with smiles and hugs on those Mondays when we saw each other. We were supportive of each other, joked frequently, and did our best to make it the happiest chemo room around.

It may seem odd to think of people getting pumped full of chemo joking and laughing as we struggled through it. But we did. That infusion center was a big part of our lives. Why would you not want somewhere that was so important to you to be a positive and happy place?

So that's exactly what most of us tried to make it. Some days we would have our infusion nurses cracking up as they changed our chemo drip bags. At a minimum we kept a smile on their faces and ours. It wasn't always easy, but I made every effort to do so, and in the end, I firmly believe that my positive attitude helped my body to handle those intense medications. My mental state was able to affect my physical condition. The same was true for the few patients there whose outlook was poor, just in the opposite way.

Eventually, I learned that this belief of mine (that your mental state affects your physical state) wasn't just my crazy theory—it was backed by science. Dr. Bruce H. Lipton, is a stem cell biologist, author, and leading researcher on the connections between our body, mind, and spirit. This field of study is called epigenetics.

I stumbled upon an article he wrote and then dove deeper into his website. What I read was inspiring. Dr. Lipton's scientific research at Stanford University had revealed that environment, including our mental state, affects our bodies on a cellular level.

In other words, his work scientifically proved that our mindset can have an actual physical impact on our bodies. So, that means a positive attitude can most definitely help you beat cancer! Dr. Lipton says, "The moment you change your perception is the moment you rewrite the chemistry of your body." I was fully on board with his findings and ready to let my mentality lead me in my fight.

• • •

I am an engineer by degree, a math guy. Due to that, the statistics of pancreatic cancer were very hard for me to cope with at first. Stated simply, the statistics suck. The most commonly referenced one is the one-year survival rate, which, per the American Cancer Society, is only 20 percent. Obviously not great.

At some point, I figured out a way to use my positive mindset to flip those statistics to a positive version in my head. Approximately 62,000 people in the United States are diagnosed with pancreatic cancer every year. With a 20 percent one-year survival rate, that means more than 12,000 people survive past that first year. Instead of focusing on the 80 percent who don't make it to the one-year point, I realized that being just one of 12,000 people didn't seem that difficult. That's what I shifted my focus to. I could easily be one in 12,000!

With that more positive viewpoint, beating pancreatic cancer felt much more possible. And in regard to cancer, statistics aren't just numbers, they're people. As people, as individuals, we have the ability to shift the statistics. I made the conscious decision to stay positive and be one of the individuals who was on the surviving side of those statistics instead of the majority side. I was going to be one of those 12,000!

CHAPTER 10

GETTING INTO THE FIGHT

Before I could get started with chemotherapy, we had to prepare my body to receive it. Many cancer patients have what is called a mediport installed. This small device was surgically installed beneath the skin in my chest, and once connected to the drip bag hanging next to my chair, it would create a medicinal pathway, routing the chemo and other medications right into my bloodstream.

My first round of chemotherapy was on Monday, October 12, 2020. My mind was spinning when I woke up that morning. I had so much fear of the unknown, fear of how I would respond to what I knew was going to be a difficult test both physically and mentally. Worries of the never-ending list of potential side effects spun through my brain.

Due to my continued weakness and the uncertainty of how I would handle the medicine, Katie drove me to the infusion center that first morning. Typically, a thirty-minute car ride with just the two of us would have been time to catch up on all the things each of us had going on at work and in life. But not on that drive. That drive was one of silent uneasiness.

I was also scared to be left alone at the infusion center. All I wanted was for Katie to be able to stay there with me all day. The medical space was her domain, and I wanted her to be the one to interact with the nurses and to answer the questions I would surely have. I wanted her there to keep me company, to keep me distracted with conversation, to comfort me if it got uncomfortable. I needed Katie there not just for her medical knowledge, but also because this cancer had split me in two. She's my other half, and when facing an enormous challenge like this, I knew she could help put me back together again.

While the port prepared my body for chemo, I couldn't find much instruction out there for how to prepare my mind. A few weeks earlier I had tried diving into a few books and searched for stories from cancer patients and survivors to better understand what I might expect. Not surprisingly, all I could find were stories from pre-COVID times. While the mechanics of receiving chemotherapy were largely the same, the emotional experiences they faced were drastically different from what I was about to experience.

Many cancer patients talk about how critical it is for their loved ones to be beside them on their journey, sitting next to them in the chemo chairs, playing games to distract them, bringing items to help comfort them, offering them popsicles and ice chips when needed, and keeping them in the best company possible. But my story doesn't include any of that camaraderie. I sat alone in my chemo chair. Unlike that first dark night when I received my diagnosis, there were amazing doctors and staff there to support me. But without Katie or other family or friends there, I felt completely alone as the medicine slowly dripped into my system for hours at a time. I had to drag my IV pole over to the fridge to get my own snacks when I needed to get something into my stomach. If I was cold, I had to grab a blanket from the shelf. I had to chase down the nurses or doctors myself if I had a question or needed some anti-nausea medications. I had to be my own entertainment for those long days of treatments, finding anything I could to distract myself from the poison pumping into my veins. I was an army of one.

That first day of chemotherapy was challenging and seemed to last forever. I was checked in and then ushered to the infusion room where I got to pick any open reclining chair of my choice. I took the one in the back corner, far away from the more experienced patients who had an early arrival time like I did. I didn't know how bad the day was going to get, but I knew that I didn't want to take a chance of vomiting in front of total strangers.

Minutes after I was settled into my recliner, a nurse came with my first dosage and pushed the needle through my skin and into my port. And just like that I was receiving my first dose of chemotherapy. It's a first I wish no one would have to experience, even if mine was off to an uneventful start.

Throughout the morning I didn't feel sick at all. I was mostly looking for things to occupy my mind, as I knew I'd be sitting in that chair for around seven hours. There was a TV in the corner, but it was tuned to a boring cooking show. I was still working full time, so I tried to distract myself with emails and various work projects as much as possible. I spent a little time on social media, then texted back and forth with Katie. I tried reading for a bit. But for a people person like me, it was a long boring day of minimal human interaction.

Then, in the middle of the afternoon, as the nurses switched to the last bag of chemo, it hit me. I was feeling fine, right up until I wasn't. The room started spinning, and it felt like I was on the world's fastest Tilt-A-Whirl. I'm also assuming my skin turned a drastically different color, because the second I felt it, the nurses knew what was up just by looking at me. They tried to add the anti-nausea medication bag ASAP, but it was too late. I grabbed my IV pole and sprinted to the bathroom.

I sheepishly returned to my chair after a good vomit, almost embarrassed that the chemo had gotten the better of me. I was pissed. Even though getting sick at the infusion center was a pretty normal and expected outcome, I felt as if the chemo, and in turn the cancer, had knocked me down a notch.

I was able to keep things together after that, but the spinning and sick feeling didn't stop until that bag of chemo completely emptied out into my system. As the dose finished, I could feel my ride in the chemo chair was winding down, and I started to recuperate. I was happy that my first seven-hour day in the infusion center was coming to a close.

My nurse disconnected me from the empty IV bag and presented me with a bonus prize: chemo to go. It was a pump that was literally attached to my hip via a fanny pack. I referred to this as my little pain-in-the-ass companion. Everywhere I went from Monday afternoon through Wednesday afternoon, that horrible but helpful little pain-in-the-ass device went along with me.

If you know anyone who has undergone cancer treatments, I'm sure you can understand how the continuous stream of chemo impacted me. It made me extremely tired and often nauseated. I had my favorite chair at the cancer center on Mondays, and the rest of the week I could be found in my at-home recliner, courtesy of my sweet mother-in-law. She loaned us her older and, according to my wife, very ugly recliner. It didn't match our décor at all and looked completely out of place in our living room, but that ugly chair propped me up literally and figuratively throughout the entire duration of my treatments.

I was still having horrible back pain and couldn't get comfortable at all. I wasn't getting much sleep in our bed, or on the couch, or the floor. This chair was the only place I could get a little relief. So even though Katie hated it, it became a fixture in our home for the entirety of my chemotherapy schedule. Even though everyone in the family joked about that old ugly chair, it became my safe haven.

I'd often wake up in the early hours of the morning in pain and feeling sick, so I would quietly move out to the living room and into that recliner. I would remain there all night, and usually for most of the next day, nodding off, only getting up to make the occasional dash to the bathroom to vomit. This became my regular routine over the next ten weeks. Running to the bathroom became my new form of exercise. The nausea and vomiting became such a regular part of life that it no longer fazed me, my wife, or my kids when I was sick. Except for Parker—she's self-diagnosed with emetophobia, which is an extreme fear of vomiting. She kept her distance on my pump days.

· · ·

From the time I first began to feel really sick in the summer of 2020, up through the first few rounds of chemotherapy, I had lost a lot of weight. My constant pain had really limited my appetite, and then the chemo and associated nausea made things even worse. A good healthy weight for me was somewhere around 175 pounds. When I started my chemotherapy treatments, I was already well below that. For the first month or so of chemo, my weight continued to drop rapidly.

As a former wrestler, I had built a habit of hopping on the scale every morning for most of my life. And while I tried not to obsess over my weight, I kept watching the pounds fall away. I tried desperately to offset my losses by forcing myself to eat and supplementing my diet with protein shakes. It was not working. I'm not a picky eater. But as I struggled through the pain, illness, and chemo, absolutely nothing tasted good. Eating became a chore, and it frequently took more effort than I could summon. It was a vicious cycle. I needed food for energy to help me fight, but I couldn't find the energy or strength to even consume the food I so needed.

I vividly remember the morning I saw 128 flashing back up at me like a warning signal on the scale. That was a defining moment, the moment where I really started worrying whether I was going to make it. I was so scrawny that I couldn't even look at myself. I would intentionally look away from the large mirror in our bathroom as I stepped into the shower. The sight of my withering body scared the hell out of me.

This cancer was taking too large a toll on my body. I was suddenly convinced I was going to die, and soon. I remember thinking I could not drop any lower. I clearly remember the conversation with myself: If I go below 125 pounds, that would be the point of no return. In my head, three more pounds represented the only thing between me and certain death.

As I stepped off the scale and into the shower that morning, I began crying uncontrollably. If I could have stepped out of my body that day, I could imagine looking down on myself, a near skeleton of a human body, slouched and crying while the water washed over me. I must've looked like I was on death's door, one small step away from the end.

The tears I released that day represented a lot of things. They represented the fear that I'd been trying to hide from. The fear of dying. The fear of losing the fight. The fear of losing to cancer and leaving my family to mourn. They also represented a turning point, a point of letting all that fear go. And they eventually represented me falling back into my faith, trusting in God's plan, and committing to fight with all I had for as long as I possibly could.

There are two main places those of us fighting cancer are able to really let our emotions out. One is in the shower; the other is in the car while driving alone. Those are the two places where you don't have to worry about one of your kids or your spouse seeing that you aren't really as tough as you like to pretend. Those are the only two places you can completely let it all out in complete privacy.

All those tears were the release I needed to deal with that extremely low number I saw on the scale. As the flow of tears slowed down, the heaviness of my situation seemed to lift off my chest just a little. Once I completed that extended shower, I found a way to collect myself and decided that it was time to really start to fight. I could not lose any more weight. I had to find a way to gain.

But then I received a miracle! A very strange miracle, but most definitely a miracle. About a week after my shower scene, in the middle of the night, I woke up hungry. Not just a little hungry, like I could maybe force down a small midnight snack or something—I was starving, and it was one of the best feelings in the world. I had the most specific and strong craving ever. I was still mostly asleep, in a dreamy fog, but that craving was crystal clear: I had to have a Jimmy John's sandwich (a Jimmy John's club sandwich to be specific), and my life quite literally depended on it.

The next morning, I told Katie about this semiconscious craving, and she was so excited at the thought of me being able to eat that she made immediate plans to go to Jimmy John's on her lunch break. This was breaking news in the house of Mysen, so she made a quick Facebook post about it before heading off to work. Before noon, multiple sandwiches were delivered to my door by neighbors and friends who were apparently also very excited by the news. And while I could only eat one of those sandwiches that day, I ate the entire thing in one sitting. It was a huge victory and a giant step forward in my recovery.

That was the breakthrough I needed with my appetite and weight loss issues. After that first sandwich, I was able to regain my hunger and slowly made my way back to a normal cycle of eating. I was able to add healthy weight, and before too long I was back up into the 160s. My ascent back to a healthy weight wasn't exactly "freaky fast," but I never dropped back down to those scary numbers on the scale after that miracle Jimmy John's craving and delivery.

• • •

After a few rounds of chemo, my treatments became more of a routine—one that I was able to adapt to and accept as the best chance of winning my battle. I fully embraced the process. I wouldn't say I enjoyed my chemotherapy treatments, but I can say that I did start to look forward to my treatment days in a way. Receiving chemotherapy, regardless of the nasty side effects, meant I was fighting back. Sitting in that chair meant I was being the aggressor and not just letting the cancer decide what happened to me. Chemo treatments were the best way for me to fight. So, as rough as they were sometimes, I embraced those treatments. I was in the fight.

Even in my weakened state, I was able to dig deep to find strength and courage, often by looking outside myself and really examining and analyzing the situation. I felt alone without Katie by my side, but I wasn't alone.

That was largely because there were about five of us patients going through our treatments together. We all had different types of cancer and were in different stages of our fights, but we were all in the same boat. None of us had the option to have a loved one support us through our treatments. So, there we were, bodies stationed across the room as we received our doses of the "good poison." Without our loved ones around us, many of us had to learn how to lean on each other. We were a varied mix of age, culture, background, and cancer diagnosis. But we were all bonded via our parallel treatment schedules.

One lady who always sat near me had lung cancer that had spread to many of her other organs. She was a lifelong smoker who had expressed much regret to me about her past decisions. Based on our many discussions, I understood she had lived a difficult life. She was Stage 4, and her prognosis wasn't very good. But she always gave off so much positive energy, despite her grim status. She had an incredible aura about her. She always had a hug for me, every single time we walked into that room together. We had lived very different lives yet had developed a close bond in the infusion center.

Another woman had lupus. Lupus is a disease I only minimally understood prior to meeting her at our infusion treatments. It is a chronic inflammatory illness that occurs when a person's immune system attacks their tissues and organs. Some people, like this woman, are given infusion treatments similar to what cancer patients receive. She was on the same schedule as I was, always there on the same days and for similar timeframes, getting similar meds as the rest of the cancer patients in the room. She was very diet-focused, trying to stay as healthy as possible to offset her disease. She was always offering me healthy snacks and was great at noticing when any of the rest of us in the room were a little more down than normal. She did her best to pick us back up a little.

There was an older, very tranquil gentleman. He always looked a little overdressed for a cancer treatment. Most of us dressed for comfort; he typically was in no less than business casual attire. He was exceptionally polite and mostly reserved. While he typically kept to himself, he seemed to always be listening to our discussions, but rarely participated. When he did join in, it was always insightful, as if he were choosing to share his vast wisdom with us only sparingly. Despite his quiet nature, he was a key part of our little cancer team, and always there with us, even if he chose to stay to the edge of things.

There were a few others as well, who were on slightly different schedules. I was not as close to them as the regulars, but they were still part of our cancer family and joined in on our many conversations, laughs, and occasional tears.

•   •   •

All of us who battle cancer have a bond. That support group extended beyond my newfound friends in the infusion center. As I went through my battle, I leaned closely on those I knew who were fighting or who had fought cancer.

My mother-in-law, Vonda, had fought and beat breast cancer a few years before I was diagnosed. She was a huge inspiration to me, providing incredible, endless support to our family.

My cousin Staci and Katie's cousin Abby both fought and beat breast cancer at the same time I was dealing with my cancer. The support and understanding they provided was immensely helpful.

My aunt Deb also went through a battle with breast cancer that overlapped my battle. We were able to help each other along the way as well.

My friend Corey had previously beaten a very rare cancer, overcoming insurmountable odds. His story and support gave me a huge boost along the way.

Another great friend, Greg, lost his battle with colon cancer while I was in the middle of my battle. Greg had been a huge inspiration, as he'd fought his battle for over ten years before we lost him. He had been through it all and never let it drag his attitude down. He was a true inspiration and is greatly missed.

My good friend, Coach Jay Smith, was another cancer survivor who was a huge supporter. His pep talks are world class and always helped to give me a boost when I needed it the most.

There were three fellow cancer warriors who were especially important to me in the fight, as they were very close to me and going through it at the same time. The first was my buddy Travis. We coached sports together and had become good friends. As we were dealing with some of the same challenges, he became a friend I could go to who could relate to my experience. His support became something I relied on. His story inspired me, as he had shown me that you can continue to coach and be actively involved in your kids' activities while fighting cancer, and then he showed me that it can be beaten.

The next was my friend Bob. Bob and I had not met prior to cancer, even though he lived only a few miles away. Bob was diagnosed with pancreatic cancer one month to the day after I was, although he was unfortunately diagnosed at Stage 4. Bob and I were introduced shortly after our diagnoses. We immediately got along.

We had a lot in common, both in how we chose to fight cancer and in our general views and beliefs. We were introduced by mutual friends who thought we might be stronger together in our shared cancer fight. Those friends were correct, as we quickly developed a true friendship and leaned on each other as we went through our treatments and cancer struggles in tandem.

Unfortunately, we lost Bob in January of 2022. As a revered officer in our local sheriff's department, he showed me the impact one can have on their community. Giving back to my community to a level even close to his has become a goal of mine. I miss him and continue to fight my battle to honor his legacy. I wish I'd had the opportunity to thank him one last time. Great men like him don't come along very often, so I'm glad that I had the chance to have him in my life, even if only for a short time.

My third cancer warrior in the fight with me was my little buddy Tate. Tate is the teenage son of Vince, my very good friend from high school. Tate was diagnosed with leukemia at age thirteen, around the time of my diagnosis. We had never met at that time but connected through Vinny as we both tried to cope with our cancers. Tate became one of my biggest inspirations. The strength with which he fought cancer at such a young age was amazing to me. Tate motivated me. I really wanted to inspire him in return. Tate was the reason I was able to get a run in or hit the heavy bag on some of my really bad days, as I wanted him to see my fight in the hopes it would inspire him to keep fighting as well. Cancer sucks for everybody, but it does not seem fair to me that someone as young as Tate should have to deal with it. But as bad as it was, he always fought it head-on and with an extremely positive attitude.

As a sophomore, at age fifteen, in the middle of his battle, Tate decided to play tennis competitively for the first time on his high school team. That fall, on a day when he had a spinal tap, multiple forms of chemo treatments, and a round of steroid injections, he won a doubles match with his partner to help his team get a win. Seeing his grit, I could not allow myself to give anything less. Tate is currently in remission. I can't wait until his battle is just one small part of his past—something that he beat, and something that made him stronger. I can't wait to see where life takes him, and I thank him for his constant inspiration along the way.

•　•　•

I started to look forward to my chemo days. I told myself that the chemo was kicking the tumor's ass, that it was my ally. Going to the infusion center meant the chemo and I were fighting back against the cancer; it was how I could win. I was in a war, and that toxic chemo was the biggest weapon in my arsenal.

Every other Monday I would wake up, write a positive Facebook update post about my fight, put a smile on my face, and go take care of business. I truly became a warrior going into battle. The cancer was my enemy, and I was determined to win my war against it. I was going into that battle powered by positivity and faith, armed with my ally: the chemo. My chemo days were the days I was going on the offensive, taking it to the cancer instead of letting the cancer come after me.

I also made it a goal to always be the most positive patient there. That sounds strange, I know. But in my heart, I strongly believed that exuding unwavering optimism would help me in the battle, and maybe help some of those other patients at the infusion center who were struggling even more than I was. So, there I was, Mr. Positive, greeting everyone with a smile with every walk to my recliner.

I wasn't trying to minimize the severity of my situation, or of those around me, with my excessive positivity. Our circumstances were obviously dire. But I had a choice. I chose to face it armed with positivity. I just couldn't allow myself to stay stuck in the shock of a horrible situation. By pushing myself to be upbeat and optimistic, even when I was feeling really bad, I was able to take the emphasis off me for moments at a time, and I could be a bit more like my old self, who liked to focus on others.

My days there started and ended with a hug for the nurses who helped me make it through each of those treatments. They became more than my nurses; they became friends and people I relied on. They did all of that and more for me, so the least I could do in return was keep a smile on my face, make a few funny comments throughout the day to try to make them laugh, and treat them as pleasantly as possible, as they so deserved.

At a minimum, they were getting a huge smile along with a cheery "good morning" from me. I frequently shared stories of the crazy things my kids were up to, which usually got some laughs. I always asked how they and their families were doing, and made sure every conversation was about more than just my cancer. Really, I just tried to be cordial, considerate, happy, and engaged with them, which unfortunately is not the way very sick people often treat medical staff.

. . .

Approximately ten weeks after the start of my chemotherapy, I had my fifth and final round of FOLFIRINOX. Those ten weeks kind of felt like ten years. But I somehow survived, and in some ways even thrived, through it all. A few days after that final treatment, I had my CT scan to evaluate if the chemo had worked to shrink the tumor, and if I could be a candidate for the Whipple procedure. That Whipple procedure was our one and only hope, the thing we had been praying would become an option. The results of that CT scan would tell us if our prayers would be answered. After a few very long days of nervously waiting, the results were in.

The chemotherapy had reduced the size of the tumor some. It was still very close to my superior mesenteric artery, but my surgeon believed that it had shrunk enough that there was at least a chance it could now be removed. This was the news we had been praying for. But like everything so far in my cancer journey, it wasn't that simple.

The radiologist noticed some abnormalities on my liver but couldn't determine what exactly they were. If the spots were cancer that had spread, that would mean my cancer status had transitioned to Stage 4 and I would no longer be a candidate for the Whipple procedure. Another biopsy was in order, this time to look at the spots on my liver. I was headed back to the hospital for another surgery, under anesthesia for the fifth time in just five months. We were at another critical turning point.

I was starting to feel like we were never going to catch a break. If the cancer had spread to my liver, the fact that the tumor had shrunk didn't matter. All of that chemo I had endured would be for naught. It felt like we had taken two steps forward only to take three steps back. I was fighting to stay optimistic but was starting to feel like the odds were stacked too steeply against me.

I was looking for my inspirational Disney movie happy ending. I was a good guy who had been dealt a difficult hand with a cancer diagnosis that felt like a death sentence. I went through the adversity of being sick and the intense chemotherapy treatments with my head held high. If it was like the movies, I was now supposed to be getting cleared for my Whipple surgery, which would in turn be a complete success, and I would be declared cancer-free. But instead, we were facing the potential of being dealt another bad hand.

As you can guess, I was extremely stressed out as I was being prepped in the pre-op room. It felt like the next few hours were a make-or-break point. Everything (and I mean everything) was riding on what we would find in this biopsy. But I had learned a lot already in my brief battle with cancer. I knew the stress and worry wouldn't help. So, I put a smile on my face, convinced myself to stay positive, and prayed. Just like I had after my diagnosis, I repeated Proverbs 3:5–6 and the phrase "*faith* over fear" repeatedly until the anesthesia kicked in and I fell asleep.

•   •   •

It seemed like two more months had passed after the biopsy, but only two days later we got the results we had been anxiously waiting for. The test results were negative. The spots were noncancerous. I was finally getting the break I was looking for, and the surgeon told us the Whipple surgery could happen.

My body needed at least four weeks to recover from chemotherapy before the doctors would even touch me. The Whipple procedure is a very long and difficult surgery that would put my body to the ultimate test, so I would need to be as healthy as possible. The surgery is extremely complex; there are very few surgeons in the world who can even perform it. This was a high-risk opportunity I was getting.

I was told by the surgeon that there was only a 50 percent chance that he would be able to remove the tumor. The other 50 percent chance was that he could get in there and find it was still too engaged with the artery and he would be unable to get it out. He expected the surgery to take somewhere between eight and ten hours. There was a small chance I may not survive the surgery at all. The surgery was my only chance for my happy ending, so I saw no other choice but to proceed. A coin flip chance of success and being cancer-free was good enough for me. We were ecstatically all in and scheduled the surgery for January 13, 2021.

• • •

My physical condition had started to improve some by the time we set that surgery date. My weight had come up significantly. The severe back pain that had plagued me for most of the year was completely gone. The chemo, as rough as it had been, had done its job and shrunk the tumor enough that it was no longer pressing on those nerves, meaning I was finally pain-free. Without the pain, and with the added strength from the extra weight, I was able to start working out a little again in early December. Things were improving. I started to genuinely feel good again. I had hope.

I knew I had to prepare my body, so I went into fight camp mode. My workout schedule went from basically nothing to intense and almost daily as soon as I knew that I could get the procedure. I knew that the results of that surgery would mostly be in the hands of God and my surgeon but felt that I had to do everything I could to prepare my body and my mind for that day. I was going to ensure that I was ready.

I prepared for the surgery like I was some cancer-stricken version of Mike Tyson prior to a heavyweight title fight. I started running on the treadmill again and hitting the heavy bag regularly. Working out again not only helped me physically, but it did wonders for me mentally as well. It felt so good to fight back. Training hard like that made me feel alive. I also started to post updates of my workouts and videos of them on Facebook. I started receiving so much positive feedback from people encouraging me. It helped me so much—way more than I could have even imagined.

I had approximately five weeks to train, from when I started working out again until my surgery date, and I took full advantage of that time to prepare as best as I could. By mid-January, I found myself mentally, spiritually, and physically ready to face the most significant and scary event of my life.

CHAPTER 11

FINDING A WAY TO FIGHT BACK

After I was first diagnosed, my body was a mess. I was down approximately fifty pounds. I was experiencing horrible back pain. I was exhausted all the time. I was very, very weak. But once the chemo started working, my pain ceased, and my weight started to return a little.

At first, I was scared to work out again, considering all my body had been through. My head was filled with fears of all the things that could go wrong: pulled muscles, broken bones, or, worst of all, a bruised ego. But once I committed to and survived my first workout, I was all in. I had a concrete, short-term goal to be physically ready for my Whipple procedure and a longer-term goal to strengthen my body for all that cancer was going to hit me with. I was on a mission. Working out was officially a significant part of my cancer-fighting strategy.

Working out after getting smashed by chemo may seem counterintuitive, but for me it became a must. The chemo makes you feel like shit, obviously. That meant I really had an easy excuse to not work out. But that need to overcome what cancer was trying to control in my life was exactly why working out became mandatory for me.

If I let it drag me down and keep me from pushing through, I was letting the cancer win. Screw that. That was not an option for me. I was too competitive to let it win that easily. So down to the gym I would go, and the whole time I worked out I would feel like I was giving a huge "F you" to the cancer. I was not passively going along for the shitty ride cancer was taking me on. I was instead grabbing the bull by the horns and saying, "I'm here, let's fight." Cancer wants to take all the control, but hitting the gym allowed me to take a little of that control back. It put me in the driver's seat, and that was exactly what I needed in my battle.

•   •   •

We'd bought a Peloton bike in late 2019, prior to the pandemic. I had used it a lot during my early 2020 weight loss journey. When I started to feel a little better around the end of my first chemo cycle in late 2020, I decided the bike would be a good place to start my cancer workouts. It quickly became one of my three or four main workouts each week. The bike provided me with a great cardio workout in a relatively short time. The rides were perfect for getting my body's strength and endurance back up to a level I needed to counteract the negative effects of the cancer and my treatments.

Beyond the great cardio impact, I really enjoyed that the platform is used by a lot of people. There are participants from all over the world. That means in any given class, and at any given time, there are typically hundreds or even thousands of other people riding in the same class as you. It was exactly what I needed to drive me. I was racing other Peloton members from all over the world every time I got on it. In my mind, I was also racing against my cancer. That was a never-ending race. But when I was kicking ass and really crushing it on the bike, I felt more strongly than ever that I was beating it.

I also added running back into my workout regimen. I had loved running since I was young. It felt great to add runs back into my life.

As it was winter, my runs occurred mostly on the treadmill in our home gym. Most were in the two- to five-mile range. Not marathons by any means, but enough distance and speed to give me a good cardio workout and help me physically in the fight.

When the weather improved, I added outdoor runs, mostly through our neighborhood, to my routine. Running outside, versus on the treadmill, adds a whole new aspect. I started to appreciate the little things on my runs way more than before cancer. The sun on my face, the sound of the birds, the occasional smiling neighbor in their yard, and the smell of the fresh air all had a much bigger impact on me. It wasn't just a workout anymore; it was an opportunity to truly enjoy and appreciate nature and everything life has to offer.

I also dove much deeper into my thoughts on those runs, which I didn't do prior to cancer. I began to use that time on the treadmill or road for serious reflection. I had many talks with God and some intense positive self-talks. Running became an activity that allowed me to calibrate myself physically, mentally, emotionally, and spiritually.

While my running was mostly a training tool against cancer, I was also able to mix in a few races over those first few years after diagnosis. One of the most important was the PanCAN PurpleStride five-kilometer race, which is an annual event organized by the Pancreatic Cancer Action Network to raise funds for research. The event raises hundreds of thousands of dollars every year. It occurs simultaneously in sixty major cities across the United States. But when I ran it, COVID caused the event to occur virtually.

As their cause was also the biggest cause in my life, I chose to be a team captain and recruit family and friends to donate and to run with me. This gave me two competitive outlets, one of course being the race, and the other being the fundraising competition against other teams that took part in the event. The team name we chose was Dusty's Purple Pack. I was extremely humbled when more than fifty family members and friends joined my team and many more donated. Our team was able to raise thousands of dollars and finish in the top five in fundraising for the entire state of Michigan.

On race day, even though it was a virtual event, friends and family drove from all over the state to join me locally in our run. The adrenaline of receiving all that love and having all those people show up pushed me to a run time that I was pretty proud of. I had set a somewhat aggressive goal of breaking 25 minutes, and I wasn't sure I was going to be able to do it. That was a pretty fast time for my age, even without cancer and chemo treatments. But the love I felt on that day from people far and wide pushed me. I ended up finishing that 5k race in 24 minutes, 58 seconds. I beat my goal time. Barely, but I beat it.

I followed up with a few additional virtual 5k races over the course of that year. Those races inspired me to push my running even further. I decided to attempt a ten-kilometer trail race. It was my first in-person race in years, and my first race of that distance since high school. Not only was the weather horrible, with temperatures in the low thirties and freezing rain, it was also an oral chemo treatment day for me. But after waking up and taking my chemo pills, I drove to the race and ran a very respectable sub 55-minute 10k.

Running an in-person race again was amazing. Training for it did amazing things for my body in my cancer fight. Of equal importance, the in-person aspect of the race did wonders for my mental state. The running community is one-of-a-kind. It is phenomenal. Runners are a group of like-minded people who all put a strong focus on supporting each other. Yes, we all compete. But for the most part, we compete against our personal time goals and not against each other. Each runner wants every other runner to achieve their personal goals almost as much as they want to achieve their own. It's a huge supportive community.

For this particular race, I thought it would be funny to wear a shirt that said, "Fighting Cancer, Going Through Chemo, and Still This

Sexy!" Pre-race, I got a lot of compliments and laughs over that shirt and a few questions about my health, which I gladly answered. Post-race, I got a whole lot of congratulations, high fives, and tear-filled hugs from that amazing running community. Those other runners, none of whom I knew, filled my heart with love. In this case, what running did for my spirit far outweighed what it did for me physically.

I also added my third and probably favorite type of workout to my routine: boxing. In our home gym, I had a heavy bag, an aqua bag, a speed bag, and mirrors. I typically did around ten rounds on the heavy bag or aqua bag, along with some additional work on the speed bag. On days that I needed to go lighter, I would incorporate shadow boxing in front of the mirrors instead of hitting the bags.

Boxing was great for me. It's a great cardio workout, and throwing the various punches into the bag requires full muscle engagement. Physically, it's very challenging and fun. The bigger part for me was the mental aspect. Boxing while having cancer was like I was literally fighting the disease. I often vividly imagined my tumor on the heavy bag as I punched it. Sometimes it made me so emotional that I cried as I hammered away at the bag. Having cancer can make you angry. Boxing gave me a way to take that anger out in a positive way. It was my release. It became my go-to workout when cancer pushed me to my highest stress levels.

I posted regularly on Facebook about many of my workouts. It was my way of showing family and friends that I wasn't giving up. That I was fighting back against cancer in every way that I could. My boxing workout posts typically received even more response and support than the others. I think my friends and family saw the symbolism as well. I sometimes posted videos of me going through one of my heavy bag workouts. Those videos showed me beating on the bag with everything I had. It was symbolic of what I was trying to do to cancer. I believe people understood that and were inspired by my fight. They responded to those posts with so much love and support. That in turn inspired me to keep fighting.

The one workout that I wasn't able to do much of was lifting weights. I had lost a lot of strength. I might have been able to lift with significantly lower weights than I was used to, but I wasn't willing to accept doing so much less. So instead of lifting weights, I settled on daily push-ups to hold onto as much muscle as possible. I downloaded an app that allowed me to keep count of my push-ups. I started doing around twenty-five at a time, once a day. But soon, I was regularly doing 100 or more per day. And I was doing that five or six days a week. In one month in early 2022, I was able to do more than 3,000 push-ups, averaging over 100 per day for the entire month.

When cancer really had me beat down, I would frequently settle for much easier workouts. I would often go for walks around the neighborhood. Many times, Katie or one of the kids would join me on those. While they weren't intense workouts, they were helping me physically, along with giving me some memorable moments with my family. As we walked, we had some deep conversations. In many ways, these "easy" walks were some of my most memorable workouts through all of it.

CHAPTER 12

FOCUS ON WHAT YOU'RE FIGHTING FOR

In any challenge you face in life, there must be something that drives you to overcome it. We need a purpose. None of us enjoys suffering, and we're not going to struggle through those tough times without having something to focus on and give us a reason to keep going. The same is true when battling cancer. Without something to fight for, I'm not sure it would be possible to stand up to that monster.

For me, the primary reason was my family. The thought of me dying before the age of fifty, which was a statistically probable outcome, and leaving my amazing wife a widow and my four children without a father was not something I could accept. I wasn't afraid of dying, really. I had lived a very good life and accomplished and experienced so many things already. I had checked most of the boxes on my life goals checklist. But I could in no way accept the grief and hardship I knew my death would cause my wife and kids. They were all too young to have to go through that. I just couldn't allow it.

I knew I had to do everything in my power to ensure that I postponed that point for them for as long as possible. Every time I was struggling through a chemo round or just having a bad cancer day, I would focus on my family. I would think about all the amazing experiences we'd had and how I needed to have more, and even better, experiences with them.

I set family-based goals to give myself targets to still be around for. I had a list of short-term, mid-term, and long-term goals. In the worst of my days, I even had immediate timeframe goals like just being able to find the strength to attend one of the kids' sporting events that night or summoning the strength to climb the stairs to tuck Grady into bed. There probably aren't many people who've patted themselves on the back for being able to walk up one flight of stairs to tuck in their son, but I have. And after patting myself on my back, I would usually smile a little in gratitude for having had the opportunity to achieve that goal.

I learned to genuinely appreciate every one of those simple, normal, everyday activities. I would sometimes hear parents at a volleyball or basketball practice complain about having to spend their night in a gym while their kid practiced. That was something I never did. I knew there were only so many of those I would get to be at, and that number could be a pretty low one. I took every opportunity to be at a practice, be at a game, tuck them in, or even just drive my kids to a friend's house.

My shorter short-term milestone goals mostly focused within the next year, like the kids' upcoming school and sports activities. Early after diagnosis, I had a goal of making it to see Grady's first travel basketball game, since he had not yet started playing competitively. Check.

I really wanted to see Parker's first high school volleyball game. Check.

I wanted to watch Landon play his first season of high school golf as a sophomore. Check.

I wanted to see Tristen play a few seasons of college basketball. Check.

I wanted to see him make his first college basket. Check.

I made it to see all those things. I was able to give myself a "carrot" that drove me to push through the hard days.

My mid-term goals are within approximately five years. Some of these I've already made it to, and some are yet to come. While the likelihood of reaching all these goals is definitely lower based on the pancreatic cancer survival rates, they're all things that are critical for me to see, so I'm determined to beat the bleak survival odds. These goals include some major life milestones for my family. I didn't want to miss Landon graduating high school or Tristen graduating from college. Both of those events happened in 2023, approximately two-and-a-half years after my diagnosis. I am happy to say that I was able to see both of their graduations.

I'm now chasing my yet-to-come mid-term goals. Parker will be getting her driver's license. Grady will start middle school and also start playing middle school sports. These are milestones to be here for. Katie's family practice has continued to grow rapidly over the years, and I can't wait to see where she takes it in my mid-term timeframe. These mid-term goals are all upcoming life-altering events for my family, and I intend to give every effort to be here to see them.

My long-term milestone goals are things beyond five years. The pancreatic cancer five-year survival rate is only 12 percent. Making significant plans beyond five years seems a little crazy. But I'm doing it anyway.

I have a goal to see Parker graduate high school, which won't happen until 2026. I have also set a goal to see Grady take part in high school sports, which can occur around 2027 at the earliest. I also want to be there to help him learn to drive when the time comes.

I set an even longer-range goal of seeing him graduate high school and head off to college, which will happen in 2031. I have a goal of seeing Landon graduate college, likely to happen around 2028, around the same time I'd like to see Tristen graduate med school and become a doctor.

I have even longer-term experiences I want to see beyond all those. Who doesn't want the chance to have major life events like seeing your kids get married, walking your daughter down the aisle, maybe even becoming a grandparent someday? Those things are in my long-term goals as well. And all those goals give me something to strive for.

The final long-term goal is Katie and me retiring somewhere warm. Before cancer, we used to watch a reality show called *Caribbean Life*. People on the show purchased retirement homes on various islands and beaches across the Caribbean. We used to talk about which island we'd settle on. When cancer hit, that dream was taken away from our hopes. But after a while, I decided there was no reason I couldn't be the one who truly upends those pancreatic cancer statistics and makes it to an amazing retirement on some exotic beach with my beautiful wife. Why shouldn't I be? So that has become my ultimate cancer-defying long-term goal that I'm determined to achieve.

CHAPTER 13

MY SUPPORT SYSTEM STARTS WITH FAMILY

Cancer is a beast of an adversary. Faith and positivity laid the foundation I needed to fight it. But I needed more. That "more" ended up being the strong support system I had behind me. I was blessed beyond belief in that regard. From the moment I was diagnosed, my family and friends stepped up in a huge way to support me in every way imaginable. Without them, I don't think I would've made it.

That support system started first and foremost with the love of my life, my wife Katie. She was my rock. Unlike most others, she was witness to 100 percent of my journey. She of course saw me trying to make the best of things and exhibiting a positive attitude most of the time, but she also saw all the bad stuff too. She saw the really sick times and the times I cried uncontrollably out of pain and fear.

She was there through every minute of the battle. She never wavered through any of it. She handled the good days and bad days equally, taking a level approach to it all. She seemed singularly focused on getting our family through it and steadily marched forward even though I know my cancer had a huge impact on her as well. Somehow she was able to push the pain that cancer was inflicting on her personally to the background so that she could focus on our kids, and on me. She was, and is, truly amazing.

I guess I shouldn't have been surprised by her ability to handle this difficult situation. She has shown me since the day we met how incredibly strong and amazing she is. She has proven over and over again how she can handle whatever is thrown at her without even flinching. She had our first child, Tristen, at just nineteen years old. She managed to get her first degree in nursing while raising him alone and working a part-time job to support him.

After we met and got married, she continued to pursue additional degrees while having our three other children. She completed her bachelor's degree in nursing while Landon was a baby, her master's degree in nursing to become a nurse practitioner while Parker was a baby, and finally her doctorate in nursing shortly after Grady arrived.

When she got frustrated by the lack of patient focus at the large office she was working at, she did what very few nurse practitioners in Michigan had ever dared to do: She started her own thriving patient-centered family practice from the ground up. She had never run a business before and wasn't really sure how to, yet she figured it all out. She ignored all the naysayers, plowed forward with the same level approach that she uses to face all challenges, and made a practice to be proud of. Her patients are very lucky to have her. I was fortunate enough to have her as my own in-home caregiver through the worst that cancer had to offer. I saw firsthand the amazing care that all her patients received.

She forced me from day one of our cancer journey to live life as normally as possible. She would not accept any less than the most I could give. In those early days with cancer, "as normal as possible" was sometimes just getting out of the recliner and joining the family at the table for dinner for a few minutes. But as she continued to help and push me, we were able to get back to a mostly normal life, except for the frequent doctor visits, scans, and treatments. I was able to work full time, work out regularly, attend almost all the kids' various activities, and help with daily chores around the house.

Through it all, Katie was my superhero caregiver. There were times she had to do everything. It was a lot! She had to take care of me completely in the worst of it. That meant taking me to all my appointments, making sure I took all my meds, managing my lack of appetite and trying to find things I could eat, and being my emotional crutch to keep me fighting.

When I was at my worst, it was like a full-time job being my caregiver. But on top of that, she was also being the primary parent to four very busy kids. She was still working two full-time jobs, as a university professor and running her family practice, which was still growing at an incredible rate. Plus, she did all the things I normally did for our family. She was doing double-duty and then some. And during that time, she also helped me grow in my faith, stay positive, pushed me to get up and moving as much as possible, and was at times the primary interface to my medical team. She did it all. Without her, there is absolutely no way I would have survived my battle.

She was also the role model and example that our kids mirrored regarding my cancer. Following her lead, each of our four children were also a main part of my support system. Each of them found ways to help me through the battle, and in some cases didn't even realize how important that was. Each supported me in a way that befit their own unique personalities, which made it even more beneficial.

At the time of my diagnosis, Tristen was attending school and playing basketball at Lake Superior State University. Lake State is approximately five hours from our home, right on the Canadian border in Michigan's Upper Peninsula. Having him move so far away was very difficult for us, but he was chasing his dreams and we were proud of him.

But when cancer hit, Tristen made the very tough decision to end his basketball career with a few years of eligibility remaining and move back home to finish his studies at our local college, Oakland University. He never made a big deal of that decision, but to me it was huge and meant more than I could ever tell him. Having our entire family of six under one roof as I fought my battle made the fight seem more possible. He gave me strength when I needed it. As a young adult, he understood my battle a little more than the younger ones, and somehow knew just how to pick me up when I needed it the most. He made a very adult and selfless decision that very few twenty-one-year-olds would have made. His selflessness and family-first focus helped me more than he will ever know.

Landon's support typically involved his awesome sense of humor. Laughter truly is the best medicine, and there were many times when I was at my worst with chemo sickness that he would somehow find a way to make me laugh. And not just chuckle, but laugh until my stomach hurt. I could be lying in the recliner, barely able to keep my eyes open from the meds, but there he was doing or saying something hilarious. That is a rare gift, and one that he has in abundance. I know he didn't even realize how much it was helping me; he was just being his normal funny self. Whenever I was at a low point, he somehow knew it was time to turn it on. Landon's ability to make me laugh through my battle, regardless of how bad I felt, is the greatest gift a cancer warrior could ever receive. I hope he never stops doing that for me.

Parker's extremely caring nature meant she was very in tune with how I was feeling. It was almost as if she was literally feeling the pain and sickness along with me. That big heart of hers and her tendency to worry made it hardest on her when I got sick, as every little struggle I went through seemed to impact her directly. I would often notice her across the room, checking on me from afar. I would have done anything to have made it easier on her.

Since she was most in tune with how I was feeling, Parker was also the one who knew exactly when I needed a little pick-me-up. That usually included a perfectly timed hug and kiss from her. She always seemed to notice right when I was feeling a little sick or down and would drop whatever she was doing to come over and grab me in a big squeeze and give me a peck on the forehead.

As the youngest, Grady had a youthful positivity and slight naiveté that made it impossible for me to ever lose hope. To him, cancer was just a small hurdle that I was going to crush. He never seemed to have the slightest thought of things getting worse. He constantly hit me with, "Once you finish beating cancer, we're going to . . ." statements. For him, beating cancer wasn't an "if," it was simply a "when." That attitude was contagious. He would talk about our future after-cancer plans and I would just smile and accept that plan as set. His belief was 100 percent, zero doubts. His attitude and confidence became a buoy to me, never allowing me to dip too low, always lifting me up.

"Mom, Dad, I think the cancer has made our lives better," Grady said out of the blue one day while I was going through my FOLFIRINOX protocol. It caught both of us off guard. Katie responded with a slightly confused look. Huh? Grady matter-of-factly continued. "Yeah, I know it sounds weird, but before, we were just, like, all doing our own thing, and we didn't really do as much together. But now we watch TV together, and we care about what each other are doing more. Like, we think about if other people are OK, and we go and check on them. We acknowledge each other more. Wait, can I use the word 'acknowledge' here? I'm trying to use big words; I think that's the right one. I just think, since we got cancer, we care about each other more."

His endless positivity and ability to find the good in even the most difficult of situations set the bar for me, showing me the attitude that I needed to adopt for myself as well.

Beyond Katie and the kids, I also had amazing support from our extended family. They stepped in immediately and went above and beyond to help us. It felt as if they had put their own lives completely on hold just to support us in our time of need.

When I was diagnosed, the kids were attending school virtually due to the pandemic. I was too sick to consistently help them with their studies, and Katie had to be at her office most days. I was barely able to do my job minimally while working from home at the time and needed to be cared for most of the time myself. My extended family stepped in and picked up all the slack. While Katie was working, one of her sisters, cousins, or her mom or dad were typically at our house, assisting the kids with their schoolwork and looking after me. This went on for months. They were always there for us, doing whatever needed to be done.

My parents and brother lived much further away and couldn't make daily drives to our house. But their support was no less important. I talked to them almost daily, and their emotional support as I first dealt with the realities of cancer was critical. They were always there to listen and cheer me up whenever I needed it. I could never thank our family enough.

I also had a strong support system surrounding me in our community and beyond. As soon as we notified everyone about my diagnosis, they all lined up to help in so many ways.

Local friends and family started a meal train so that Katie and I had one less thing to worry about. Delicious meals showed up at the house every single day. The same thing happened for many of my follow-up surgeries. Family and friends from farther away sent gift cards for local restaurants so that we could have take-out dinners. Beyond the wonderful food, the outpouring of texts, calls, Facebook messages, flowers, gift baskets, get well cards, and letters I received was mind-boggling. I had never felt so loved and supported in my entire life. It truly gave me strength and hope and helped me to fight.

Local friends and other parents at the school also stepped up enormously to help with the kids' activities and other needs. They offered to help drive the kids to their never-ending list of practices, games, and other activities. These friends also offered to host the kids at their homes regularly to allow our kids a little break from the stresses of my illness and to give me a little extra chance to rest. If one of our kids' friends was going to do something fun, their parents were usually offering to take our kids along with them. I was in awe of how much people cared for us.

We were also lucky enough to have some of our best friends living right in our neighborhood. They were more than just friends; they were friends whom I counted as family. They supported us in every way, most importantly just being there when we needed someone to lean on and talk to. They were the people we went to when we needed to get out, have a nice dinner and a few drinks, and just talk and laugh. They were the people we could open up to about what we were dealing with, and not have to hide anything. Those types of friendships are rare and a true blessing. Without them, I couldn't have made it through cancer, or life in general.

I had an additional group of friends whose support was also critical in my battle: my three college roommates, Clayton, Joel, and Matt. The four of us had an ongoing group text that mostly consisted of Michigan State sports, the various happenings within our families, our careers, and other basic day-to-day events. Not many days went by where we weren't active in that group text. That group text became my go-to distraction when cancer got the best of me. Those three had an amazing way of being able to lift my spirits without even trying. They were, and are, my brothers. I expect they had no idea how important that group text had become for my mental well-being. They were just being the great guys that they are. They gave me a space to get away from the cancer and just be with my buddies. It was as if cancer wasn't even there while I was interacting with them. Their support carried me on a lot of days. To have friends like that is a true blessing that I will never take for granted.

Too many times, I saw other cancer warriors retreat into a shell and push their family and friends away. That never made sense to me. It was the time I needed my support system the most, and I leaned on them fully through it all.

CHAPTER 14

A CAREER WITH CANCER

Early on, when it felt as if my entire world was collapsing around me, I wondered whether it was possible to manage a high-level career while in the midst of a fight-for-your-life battle with cancer. As I adapted, I discovered that for me it was indeed possible. While it was far from easy, I found a way to continue working full-time through it all.

Fighting cancer often feels like a full-time job. In many cases it forces a person to quit or take significant time off. Pausing or ending your career due to a cancer diagnosis is a completely plausible and understandable outcome, but it was not one I was willing to accept. I was fortunate and stubborn enough for that never to be the case for me. No matter what cancer threw at me, I continued to still show up and throw everything I had into my work.

I was often asked how I was able to do it, and why I did it.

At a high level, the "how'" was actually pretty simple. I just kept waking up every morning, and no matter how sick I felt, I just started my normal routine of getting ready and hopping into the home office to work. Working every day had been my routine for most of my life. It was what I did. I absolutely loved my career.

It was something I wasn't willing to give up easily, so I just kept doing it in spite of the added strain and struggles that cancer had added to my life.

Diving deeper though, there were many factors that actually allowed me to continue with my job and manage the cancer burden simultaneously. My situation was unique. The circumstances at the time of my diagnosis were ideal for allowing me to continue my career.

The existing COVID work protocols at the time had shifted my job to being fully remote. It was a blessing to not have to commute to and work in the office every day. Being able to work from the comfort of my couch in casual attire made things much easier. Being removed from the germs and illnesses of the traditional office environment was also critical for my treatments. In addition, my company was very flexible with my situation, and adjusted as much as possible to allow me to continue contributing at the highest level in spite of my health challenges. My colleagues regularly adjusted their schedules for me, and often took over tasks for me when I wasn't feeling my best. I was blessed to work for a company that respected and appreciated me enough to make accommodations that allowed me to continue unhindered in my career. My role also allowed me to dictate my own schedule for the most part, permitting me to adjust for appointments, treatments, and sick time. I was also able to catch up on any missed work at night and on weekends.

I had a unique and almost perfect situation that made it possible to prosper in my career despite cancer. For me, continuing my career was possible. It was not easy, but it was definitely possible. And I did it. That is "how" I was able to continue my career during cancer.

The "why" is actually the more important question though, and it had a multitude of answers.

I didn't have to continue to work once diagnosed. It was a choice. I had the option to take some time off and use my significant amount of accrued vacation time, FMLA, short-term disability, or long-term disability. All of those things were options to us. We had alternatives available to keep us afloat financially. So, continuing to work wasn't a "have to" for financial reasons, but it was a "must" for me in multiple ways.

First of all, I needed my career for my overall mindset. Continuing to work kept things a little more normal for me. I needed something in my life that was not cancer. I needed the distraction for a good portion of the day. My career was my normal. Focusing on it distracted me from all the negatives and challenges that cancer was slamming into my life on a daily basis. Working allowed me to be something more than just a cancer patient, which I really needed for my mental stability.

My career had always been such a big part of my life, and a huge percentage of my waking hours were devoted to it. If I let the cancer put my career on hold, it felt as if the cancer was taking that on top of all the other things it was already robbing. Although it may sound odd, I felt as if continuing my career was critical to my survival. It was a crucial battle in the cancer war that I was determined to stand my ground on and win.

Much like my workouts in the gym, my career was a tool I used to try to stay strong mentally and physically. It was a tool I used to distract myself from all things cancer. It was a tool I used to give myself wins, a way of proving that I was still in control and that the cancer wasn't beating me. The feeling I got from winning new business or completing a successful outcome with one of my customers was like the feeling I had after finishing a long run. It was the feeling of accomplishment. Accomplishment in spite of cancer. It was my way of beating the damn thing. My way of kicking cancer's ass.

Taking time off work would have been the start of a downward spiral. I couldn't allow that to happen. I couldn't give up who I was. So I refused to take any time off work. I probably took less time off work for vacations and family obligations than I did prior to my diagnosis. I was afraid to be away from my career, feeling that any time away from the job may be the start of me slipping a little closer to being just a cancer patient.

While finances weren't what drove me to keep working, it was definitely a factor. I had those other options if I had decided to take a break from my career, but those options, as nice as they were, would have had a negative financial impact on my family. I vowed that my family wouldn't have to experience any financially driven changes due to my cancer for as long as I could avoid it.

My viewpoint and math on our family financials had changed. The realization that I might not be around for the long term to provide for my family scared the hell out of me. I knew that the total amount of money I would make for my family over the course of my career was likely going to be less after I was diagnosed than what I had forecasted prior. The odds I would continue to advance in my career or live to a normal retirement age had gone way down. That made every paycheck that I could deposit into the bank seem way more significant.

Taking extensive sick time would have made that deposit smaller. Going on disability would have reduced that deposit significantly. Winning less new business would have made my bonuses smaller. I was on a mission to avoid any reductions to my financial contributions to the family. It was a goal I used to keep working, to keep fighting.

Katie could have provided for our family if I could no longer contribute, or if I was no longer around. But we had built our lifestyle around our dual incomes. We both contributed our fair share to the family financials. That is the way it was from the start of our marriage. The idea of her needing to be the sole financial contributor did not sit well with me. Again, I would have felt less than my full self if we had gotten to that point. I felt a duty to my family to contribute my fair share. It would have been possible, and we would have managed, but it would have crushed my spirit and made me feel like I was letting Katie and our family down.

Those were my "whys" for continuing my career. It's what drove me to keep getting up every morning and doing my thing, regardless of my diminished health.

. . .

Cancer changed my view of what was important in my career, and it changed it in a major way. Cancer actually helped me to find significantly more happiness in my work. It shifted my view from "I have to go to work" to "I get to go to work."

In our jobs, we typically work forty-plus hours every week. Forty hours a week is around 35 percent of the time we're awake every single week. If you add in commute time, business trips, and the extra hours put in at home, our careers are typically 50 percent or more of our waking hours. That's a huge part of our lives.

Yet so many people in this world dread going to work. They hate it. Every workday is miserable. I was one of those people at times in my career. Not always, but occasionally. Cancer changed that drastically. I realized that disliking something that comprises over half of your life was extremely counterproductive. Why would I do that? It made zero sense and just seemed silly once I was able to step back and look at things with my new cancer perspective.

We can't all have our perfect dream jobs. If we could, I would've been playing in the NHL and not working in corporate America. Most of us don't ever get that job we dreamed of. But most of us do get an opportunity to land in a career that is better than we typically give it credit for. So, we should not dread our jobs. We should find ways to appreciate the opportunities our careers give us. That is a choice. That is something cancer helped me understand and what drove a huge shift in my perspective on my career.

When something is almost taken away from you, everything changes, and you truly learn to appreciate how good things are. At first, I thought cancer was going to be the end of my career, I thought it was going to be the end of everything. But once I realized that continuing to work was actually a possibility, my view shifted.

My cancer taught me to stop and smell the roses and appreciate all the little things, all the important things, in my life. I realized I wasn't going to get to work, or live, forever. At some point, maybe sooner than I could have ever thought, it was all going to be taken away. That changed me. In every way. And in my career as well.

The thing I started to focus on and truly appreciate most was the people I interacted with every day on the job. I started to see colleagues and coworkers a little differently. They were no longer just business interactions. They were people; amazing people with interesting lives and fascinating stories who I was fortunate to know. They were people I had the opportunity to interact with, and they were a huge part of my life. What was important in my career wasn't the successes or promotions or the business wins, it was the relationships that my career allowed me to build.

I engaged more intimately with colleagues. I listened more intently as they talked about their families and personal lives. I gave them updates on my health as they caringly asked how I was doing. This became a focus, a focus that I truly engaged in with all my being. My interactions were no longer just small talk to be polite, as they sometimes had been in the past. Each interaction was a meaningful and caring dialogue centered around the relationships I had been able to build with these colleagues and customers. Those relationships gave so much to me, and hopefully I was able to give a little in return to them as well.

•   •   •

The company I worked for at the time was headquartered in Tel Aviv. The vast distance between me and most of my company didn't prevent them from supporting me in enormous ways though. When I was in the hospital after that initial biopsy, my

CEO kept in touch with Katie to stay updated on my progress and offer his support. Then, while I was at the worst of my sickness early after diagnosis, one of my coworkers in Israel, Tzachi, stepped up and supported my accounts in North America in addition to managing his own in Europe. For a while, he attended all my conference calls with customers, with me or in place of me, when I was too sick to attend.

I got nauseated and sick midmeeting once and had to quickly excuse myself and run to the bathroom. Tzachi stepped right in and led the meeting for ten or fifteen minutes until I was able to return. He was like my shadow for a few months, supporting me in the background then jumping into the forefront to lead whenever I truly needed it. Tzachi and many others like him at my company made it possible for me to continue to perform in my job.

My company also supported me in many other ways. In those first weeks after diagnosis, even before the meal train, they organized a private chef to make and deliver home-cooked meals to our home. It was amazing. The chef made whatever we requested and delivered it right to our front door. My coworkers around the globe also organized a fundraiser for me and my family. They all donated money and also gave their personal vacation days back to the company in exchange for company money donated to my family. They raised thousands of dollars to help me and my family with the expenses of cancer. Things like that really turn coworkers into friends quickly.

I also received support from my previous company, even though I'd left there three years prior. My former boss organized a collection for my family. Many of my former colleagues donated. They used the donations to provide us with a huge stack of gift cards to local restaurants. It was enough to provide us with take-out meals on the nights we didn't have dinner made at home. It was an amazing showing of support from some incredible people who I hadn't worked with in years.

•   •   •

Cancer also changed the way I approached the day-to-day activities of work. I learned to take extreme joy in achieving my daily goals and tasks, even the little ones. Each win brought happiness. Similar to how I had learned to really appreciate the little things in my family life, like being able to tuck my kids in at night, I also began to truly appreciate the feeling of accomplishment that I found in completing things in my work life, even the less significant things. I had of course also found joy in the big things, like winning a huge piece of business with a key customer. But after diagnosis, all the achievements, big or small, meant more.

I learned to check off the items on my to-do list and to take pride in that. Pre-cancer, I only viewed completing those everyday tasks as doing what I was supposed to do. I didn't see it as a significant accomplishment. But cancer changed my view on that. Checking off tasks on our lists, no matter how small they may be, should always be celebrated. We need to celebrate all our wins. We need to take the joy from each and every accomplishment and cherish it. That's what makes us tick as humans. It's what keeps us coming back. We shouldn't minimize that; we should embrace it.

When you've had days where you can barely get out of a recliner and don't have the strength to even lift a glass to your lips to take a drink, being able to do critical, and even menial, tasks is no longer taken for granted. At my worst, I had days where finding the energy and mental focus to even write a simple email was a major challenge. So, when I could do those seemingly normal work activities without such a struggle, I truly appreciated having that ability. Cancer taught me that nothing in life is guaranteed and that being good at what you do for a living is a blessing that should not be taken for granted.

What drove me in my career before cancer was different. My career had been like a competition for me. My extremely competitive nature was the main driver of the majority my career successes. I was exceedingly driven to get the highest sales totals possible, striving for the highest in my entire company. I went all out to have the highest profit margins. I had a single-minded focus on winning every negotiation. I needed to win in every circumstance. I was überfocused on climbing the corporate latter, striving to grow to the highest position and title possible, and to make the highest salary and attain the biggest bonuses. My hatred of losing was the driving force for everything in my career.

After my diagnosis, my career was no longer just about winning and advancing. That actually dropped pretty low on my list of career goals. The "stop and smell the roses" change that cancer made in my personal life also became the mainstay of my work life. Instead of needing to win, I found extreme joy in just being really good at my craft.

Cancer shifted my career focus from numbers to people in so many ways. Beyond my increased focus on relationships, I also shifted to a strong focus on helping others succeed in their careers, including my younger colleagues and even my customers. It was time for me to give back. I wanted and needed to give back. I wanted to mentor and assist the next versions of me so that they could grow and have successful careers just as I had. Helping others was now the focus: in life in general, and specifically in my work.

Even my personal wins in my career became about helping others. I started to see new business wins as a way of helping the company succeed, which allowed my company to employ many others, which helped all of those other employees to provide for their families and to live a good life. The wins and successes became all about others and less about me. That was a good feeling. And it gave me new purpose.

Everything about my career became more enjoyable and rewarding post cancer diagnosis. Going to work became a blessing, not a burden.

CHAPTER 15

A FAILED WHIPPLE ATTEMPT. WHERE DO WE GO NOW?

As 2021 started, I was ready for my Whipple procedure to remove the tumor and be done with cancer! I was feeling good: I had my six-part strategy to fight cancer in place; my faith was stronger than ever; I was extremely upbeat; I had a strong focus on being there for my family; I was working out hard and fighting back physically; I had my strong support system behind me; and I had my surgeon ready to go. Things were looking up.

I continued my pre-fight training camp–style workouts as we transitioned into the new year. I was going strong with heavy bag, running, and biking workouts almost daily. It was amazing how far I had come in the few months since I was diagnosed. I was starting to feel like a badass cancer warrior! As my January 13 surgery approached, I was completely prepared and 100 percent sure that I was about to be cancer-free and moving on with life.

The night before the surgery, Katie and I stayed at a hotel close to the hospital. As much as I had prepared physically and mentally, I was still more scared than I had ever been in my life. I prayed endlessly as I lay in that hotel bed and didn't sleep very much at all. But the next morning, I pulled myself together as best as I possibly could, forced a positive attitude, and convinced myself everything was going to be all right.

In pre-op, I ramped up my positive attitude, which helped push the fear aside. I made jokes and small talk with the nurses. I set my usual goal: making staff members laugh or smile. As the first medications they gave me began to kick in, my jokes became even funnier (at least to me). Then, before I knew it, it was time.

This was not a simple procedure. It was an eight- to ten-hour surgery, with only about a 50 percent chance for success. But as I was wheeled to the OR, I was confident and ready. I asked the surgical team to say a quick prayer with me, and after we did, they started the anesthesia. Five, four, three, two, one . . .

Once the surgeon cut me open and was able to see what was really going on inside me, he unfortunately realized things were worse than we had originally hoped. The tumor was still very engaged with the superior mesenteric artery, to the point that he could not cleanly resect the tumor without a significant risk of damaging the artery. Damage to that artery would have very likely resulted in my death. A consultation with an on-site vascular surgeon while I was still open on the table confirmed my surgeon's opinion. My tumor was non-resectable. So, after approximately eight hours of surgery, they closed me back up with that nasty tumor still inside me.

When I groggily awoke in the post-op recovery room, I had just one thing on my mind. I immediately asked the surgeon, who was in there checking on my status, if he had been able to remove the tumor. He almost apologetically and empathetically replied that he'd been unable to remove it. That was crushing. I'd been so confident that my cancer journey was over—that the tumor would be removed, and I could move on with a normal life. But that apparently was not the way my story was meant to go. God had a different plan for me.

I was devastated, but I had no choice but accept the reality of the situation, put a positive spin on it, and figure out my next move.

The first step in that process was getting out of the hospital as quickly as possible. Due to the length and severity of the procedure, they had projected I would have to stay in the hospital for a week or two. That timeframe was far too long for me to accept. I wanted to get out, get home, and get back in the fight.

The day after surgery, I forced myself to start walking as often as possible. It wasn't easy with the significant postsurgical pain and the insane number of tubes and drains coming out of various parts of my body, but I knew that moving was the key to kick-starting my body back into recovery. I did laps around my hospital floor many times every day. The nurses couldn't believe how soon after surgery and how frequently I was walking.

I was trying to set lap records around that floor, as if it were a competition. Each lap was making me stronger and getting me closer to going home. I was on a mission to get out of the hospital. Just four days after that major eight-hour surgery, I was discharged.

Once home, I continued my gradual recovery. For weeks I couldn't do anything beyond walking. So I kept walking. I walked a lot. I walked outside when the weather allowed and on the treadmill when the weather did not. All that walking expedited the recovery process.

I was able to convince the surgeon to allow me to start some easy running on the treadmill sooner than the recommended four to six weeks postsurgery. A mere three weeks after surgery, I ran an easy five kilometers on the treadmill. I was back. I was working out, exuding more hope than ever, and ready to move on.

I refocused on the same six-part strategy. I was back in the fight and recovering quickly. The next big step was to figure out a new treatment plan. My surgeon was adamant that a second Whipple attempt would never be possible. I wasn't willing to accept that absolute but, for the time being, decided to just accept moving on with a new nonsurgical plan to attack the cancer.

Without a surgical possibility, the new goal for me and my oncology team was simply to focus on keeping the tumor from growing or spreading to other organs, making it Stage 4 cancer. My oncology team decided that instead of going right back on the nasty FOLFIRINOX chemotherapy regimen, it would be better to try radiation.

In mid-February 2021, I started my new radiation/chemotherapy protocol. Five days a week I took an oral chemo called Xeloda (capecitabine), then drove to the radiation center for a thirty-minute session. The chemo medication was relatively mild compared to what I had become used to, and the radiation treatments were relatively easy as well. I just had to lie on the table under a machine while they targeted intense radiation beams at my pancreas.

I usually used that quiet time for some deep reflection and serious talks with God. The time on that table ended up being quite mentally therapeutic for me. The side effects of this treatment plan were not horrible, and I was able to continue living life fairly normally, working full-time and working out on occasion.

The treatments did make me very tired, though. And the repetitiveness of it made it feel a little bit like "Groundhog Day." Every day was almost exactly the same: Wake up, take the chemo pills, work for a few hours, get the radiation treatment, work for a few more hours, rest a little, and finally finish the day off with more chemo pills. I would then wake up the next day and repeat it all over again.

This radiation/chemo treatment plan continued five days a week for seven consecutive weeks—thirty-five treatments in total. I had multiple CT and PET scans over that timeframe, all of which showed positive results. The new treatment plan seemed to be working. The scans showed the tumor was not growing and even possibly shrinking a little. The scans also showed no spread to my other nearby organs. It was working as we had hoped, preventing growth or spread.

After my seven weeks of radiation were complete, I had one final PET scan. The results were as good as we could have hoped for, showing the cancer wasn't active, with some shrinkage of the tumor as well.

We were meeting our goal: no growth and no spread. But due to the significant impact radiation can have on the tissue around the cancer site and other nearby organs, it is not a treatment that could continue long term. Those seven weeks were the end of that option. I had taken all the radiation I could take, and it was time to move on to another plan.

But first, my family and I needed a vacation. The radiation regimen had exhausted me and put quite a strain on my family. Seven weeks of me being tired and worn out, unable to help around the house as much as usual, did not make things easy on them.

Since I wasn't sure how much time I had left with my family, Katie and I decided we would make it a vacation of a lifetime. We booked a seven-day trip to an all-inclusive resort in the Riviera Maya area of Mexico for early May, while I was on a little break from treatments.

We booked the nicest suite the resort had: a two-bedroom, two-bathroom suite with a full living room, dining room, two balcony patios, and a rooftop bar and deck area with our own private hot tub overlooking the ocean. That vacation ended up being exactly what I needed, and what my family needed as well. We thoroughly enjoyed our time there. The weather was perfect. The pools and ocean were amazing. We spent almost the entire vacation together, all six of us. We hung out at the pool, enjoyed the all-inclusive food and drinks, spent time at the on-site waterpark, and enjoyed all the evening entertainment as a family. It was seven days of perfection. I almost forgot I had cancer for those seven wonderful days in Mexico.

CHAPTER 16

THE FIGHT CONTINUES AND NEW CHALLENGES ARISE

Upon our return to Michigan from that awesome vacation, I had to focus in fully, because I had to step right into another treatment plan. I knew before it started that it was going to be very difficult because it was the most intense protocol possible: the FOLFIRINOX regimen again. This time, I would do eight rounds of it, with infusions every other week. My first time on FOLFIRINOX, immediately after being diagnosed, had only been five rounds. But the good news was, my health, fitness, and weight were much better as we approached this cycle. As tough as I knew it would be, I was ready.

In mid-May I went back in the chair at the infusion center for the first of my eight rounds. I was ready, but man, I was really starting to hate that f'n chair. It was the same protocol as before: I would spend seven hours at the infusion center, getting my chemo on Monday, and then go home with my little pain-in-the-ass buddy, the pump, for an additional forty-eight hours of infusions. On Wednesdays I would go back and have the pump removed, followed by one and a half weeks of recovery time. We would repeat this for eight rounds, extending over the entire summer of 2021.

That FOLFIRINOX cocktail is no joke. Most people cannot tolerate it well at all and get extremely weak and sick. But as I went through it, I forced myself to stay positive, to trust God's plan, to work out as much as possible, and to live life to its fullest despite that nasty chemo cocktail. I was lucky enough to handle it way better than most. I still faced the nasty side effects, but they didn't hit me as severely as many people on this protocol. I really feel that my positive handling of the FOLFIRINOX was a choice in a lot of ways. I refused to let the cancer, or the chemo, be the boss of my situation.

I had been fortunate to that point in my cancer journey to not lose my hair. But that summer of FOLFIRINOX, it finally started to happen a little—not to the point that I was going bald or that it was even visibly noticeable to most, but leaving small amounts of hair everywhere I went was annoying.

One night while our family was having dinner at the home of some friends, I was describing the annoyance of my shedding hair. "We should just shave it into a mohawk!" my friend Chris joked. The idea really struck a chord with me. I told him to grab his clippers, and we would do it right then and there.

It turned into a fun family experience, as Parker and Grady both got a turn with the clippers, shaving the sides of my head completely bald. Chris completed the finishing touches, lining it up to a perfect old-school mohawk. Trust me, it was quite the look for a forty-seven-year-old cancer patient.

But I loved it. I felt it completely meshed with my spirit. I was a cancer warrior, and a good warrior can definitely rock a nice mohawk. Originally, I had thought I might just leave it for a night and then shave it all off the next day. But instead, I decided to keep it, embrace it, and make it part of my warrior persona.

I was a little worried about the effect it would have on coworkers and customers. Mohawks aren't really a look you see often in the corporate world. But contrary to what I expected, almost everyone liked it and accepted it. I think everyone in my work world, just as in my personal life, decided it was the correct look for my mindset. I did joke that I had the distinction of being the only executive in the entire global automotive industry who was rocking a mohawk. It was a distinction I took pride in, though.

Overall, my chemo that summer went relatively smoothly. But of course it wasn't all roses, as chemotherapy treatments of that type rarely are. I had my bad times over that sixteen-week regimen, even though it was mostly tolerable. Again, the chemo made me extremely tired and frequently sick.

In mid-June, the chemo decided to really remind me of just how bad it could make things. After having the pump removed that week, things went downhill. I had been vomiting randomly a few times a day after my infusion, which wasn't that abnormal for me during treatments. But one morning late in the week, I got sick, and it scared the hell out of me.

Something was different and definitely not right. I came out of the bathroom and somewhat nervously told Katie that it looked like I had just puked an entire tub of coffee grounds. I was hoping this wasn't a big deal but knew that was likely not the case.

"Well, it looks like we're headed to the ER," she said calmly. That is when I first heard the appropriately coined medical term "coffee ground emesis." I learned that vomiting what looks like a tub of finely ground Folgers is a distinct sign of internal bleeding, which is obviously not a good thing.

The ER was the last place I wanted to go, but exactly where I needed to be. I had not only been afraid of having internal bleeding, but even more so that it would likely force me to pause my chemo treatments while I healed. They were my main way of fighting the cancer. A treatment pause was not something I could accept, even a short one. Fortunately, after some tests, they determined that I did not have a GI bleed. The coffee ground emesis was likely just due to some internal irritation caused by my frequent vomiting. Not a great thing, but much better than the prognosis could have been.

I survived that summer of FOLFIRINOX. And in a lot of ways, I thrived. We still enjoyed a lot of time at the lake with friends and family. I still worked out. I still worked full-time. And in the end, the FOLFIRINOX did exactly what it was supposed to. The scans continued to show no tumor growth or cancer spread. That was our ongoing goal. Almost one full year postdiagnosis, there was no cancer spread and the tumor had shrunk to almost half the size of what it was originally. Cancer had picked the wrong guy to mess with. The cancer was still in my pancreas, but I was fighting it with everything I had.

• • •

After the intense summer of the FOLFIRINOX regimen, my oncology team decided that I needed a change in treatment type. I needed an updated plan that would be a little less severe on my body. As the cancer seemed to be relatively under control, my team decided that I would next go on a maintenance chemo cycle. The maintenance cycle would be a less aggressive type of chemotherapy, with a goal of keeping my current status of an approximately 1.5 cm diameter tumor in the pancreas with no spread to other organs. My maintenance protocol could last for approximately one full year, depending on how my body responded.

I hated the term "maintenance plan." To me, maintenance sounded like we were just giving up and waiting for the cancer to win. Instead of maintenance, I chose to look at my new plan as off-season training. I decided it was like the time a boxer has between championship fights where they really have to put in the work. It's the time the fighter focuses on getting stronger and better prior to moving on to his next opponent. So, I decided to use this as a time to get in the gym and get fitter and stronger. I would focus on spending even more quality time with my family and friends while I presumably felt a little better. I would concentrate on being even more positive and trying to give back to others. And I would grow spiritually.

In September 2021, I started my new maintenance plan. The chemo I would take was the same oral chemotherapy pills I had taken during my earlier radiation cycle. I would again be on Xeloda (capecitabine), but this time at a higher dosage: five pills in the morning and five pills at night, doing two weeks on and then one week off. During radiation, I had taken three pills twice a day. Since the Xeloda didn't cause too many significant side effects during my radiation, I was expecting a relatively easy run.

Unfortunately, the increased dosage levels caused some major unexpected issues for me. The first few cycles weren't too bad at all. Just like during my previous radiation and chemotherapy plan, I was just a little more tired than normal. But at least there was no nausea or vomiting like I faced on the FOLFIRINOX. Once I got a few cycles in, though, things got rough.

One of the side effects that Xeloda can cause is hand-foot syndrome. It's similar to having a severe sunburn on your hands and feet. It can cause major skin dryness, peeling, and pain in the extremities. I did not experience this at all during my first radiation and chemo cycle. For the first few cycles of the maintenance plan, I only had very minor hand-foot syndrome. It was not a significant issue. But in late October, it started to get very bad. Eventually the skin was peeling off my hands and feet in sheets. My hands were so dry and sore I couldn't pick things up or open a water bottle. It then got to the point that I could barely walk because my feet were so bad. This was the absolute worst time of my entire cancer journey. Without the use of your hands and feet, things get pretty bleak. It forced me to be almost completely relegated to the couch, unable to do much of anything.

Things continued to get worse. The physical pain, and the immobility it caused, led to some severe mental struggles. I fell into a horrible state of depression. This of course made things difficult for my family as well. One Sunday evening, during the worst of the hand-foot syndrome struggles, I snapped at Katie about something trivial, which led to us arguing. So I did what I usually did when I needed to be alone to process things: I went for a drive in the country.

I hobbled my way to my truck on that dark and rainy night and headed for the dirt roads in the rural area not far from our home. Usually, a drive such as this one cleared my head and allowed me to get things together, refocus, and fix whatever issue was bothering me. But on this night, I could only think about the negatives: my argument with Katie and how short I had been with her, my seemingly incurable cancer, my extreme hand and foot pain and inability to walk or do simple tasks, and how sad and upset everything had me. I couldn't stop the negative thoughts, and I couldn't stop crying. As I drove down those dark, rain-soaked dirt roads, I was sucked deeper and deeper into my depressed state.

I started to speed up. I started to think that maybe everything would be better for everyone if my cancer-riddled self was no longer around. I thought that if I just ended it all, my family and friends could finally move on and not have to worry about me and my health anymore.

I continued to speed, going way too fast for the rainy conditions and narrow, tree-lined dirt roads. My scary internal dialogue continued as I sped, and I debated whether it was time to just yank the steering wheel hard and veer into the trees lining the road and end it all. I was far too close to deciding to do just that. But I didn't, thankfully. I was able to breathe, calm down a little, slow down a lot, and pull myself together.

The first tools I usually went to had been my positivity and my faith. But not in this case. Those tools eventually helped, but not in the worst of it while I was having such horrible thoughts and speeding down those dark dirt roads. While in that situation, stuck in that horrible head space, I had to use my strongest tool: my intense love for my family. I let images of Katie and the kids flow into my head. I imagined them going to my funeral and having to move on without me. I vividly visualized their grieving. I couldn't let that happen. After that scary experience, I knew I had to talk to my doctors urgently and change the regimen I was on.

•   •   •

I told my oncology team the next day that the treatment plan had to change. My quality of life at that time was simply unacceptable. I would rather have any other treatment versus not being able to live life the way I needed to live it. I needed to be able to work out, to go to my kids' activities, to move, to function. The hand-foot syndrome was not allowing for any of that. Plus, it had caused me to fall into a horrible state of depression. The team agreed that we needed to make a change. They decided to give me a month off to recover and then try the same protocol but at a lower dosage.

I had the entire month of November with no treatments at all. After a few weeks, the hand-foot syndrome completely subsided. My mental state improved as well. I had my life back. I was able to work out again. I was able to work without pain (typing on my computer had been torturous). I was back to attending my kids' sporting events. By the end of November, I was fully healed. My positive attitude was back, and all the depression had subsided. I was back to focusing on my six-part cancer-fighting strategy and more optimistic than ever.

As December began, so did my updated, lower-dosage maintenance plan. It consisted of four Xeloda pills in the morning and then four more at night—a 20 percent reduction. It also was reduced to one week on, instead of the previous two weeks on, and then one week off for recovery. This new plan was the ticket. I didn't experience the major hand-foot syndrome again and only had occasional minor hand irritation. This plan became my new normal. The side effects were manageable, and the expectation of my oncology team was that it would support my status of no growth and no spread.

And then the unthinkable happened.

CHAPTER 17

THE SEMI CRASH

In 2014, Katie had completed her doctorate and taken a new position as a professor in the nursing department at Oakland University. She had been working as a nurse practitioner at a local family practice that was part of a large corporate hospital system, but once she became a professor, she shifted to a part-time role. She managed both roles well and loved both of them. She was thriving.

By 2017, she had become frustrated with the way the big corporate hospital-based family practices were managed. Their goal was to see as many patients as possible. The focus was completely on increasing revenue, with very minimal focus on patient care. Katie wanted, and needed, to focus more on the care of her patients. That's why she had gone into nursing in the first place.

In mid-2017, she quit her job at that family practice and opened her own.

To keep the upfront capital investment minimal, she started her practice out of our home, with no office to see patients. At that time, in-home and telehealth primary care visits were not common. Most people had never even heard of it as a choice. But her practice took off, growing at an amazing rate. She saw people in the comfort of their homes. She also saw people via video conferencing and telehealth. She grew a strong base of people who loved her as their provider. And because it was her own practice, she could stand behind her primary goal of being patient-focused. She wasn't on a patient quota, pushing them out the door as quickly as possible to get the next one in the room. She took her time with her patients to ensure they received the absolute best care possible. The flexibility of it being her practice also allowed her to more easily be the best professor possible at her primary job at the university. It was the best of all worlds.

By late 2019, she had grown her practice significantly and needed an office and a staff. She found the perfect space to lease right in our little hometown of Oxford. In early 2020, she hired a medical assistant and opened the doors of her new office. I was so proud of what she had created.

When I was diagnosed in September 2020, Katie considered closing the practice to focus on being my caregiver. She was juggling multiple jobs that were all very time-consuming. In addition to being a full-time professor at a major university and running a rapidly growing family practice, she was also doing some side work as an expert witness in court cases. "Busy" did not even come close to adequately describing her life. And on top of the multiple thriving careers, she was also busy raising our four very active children and being an incredibly supportive wife to me. When I was diagnosed with cancer, it felt like something really had to give. Being a professor was her primary job and how we got our health insurance, so that was a job she preferred to not have to leave. Katie really felt that with our new situation, and the scary unknown of my upcoming battle, closing the doors of her practice might be best for all of us.

As sick as I was, I wasn't much help in the decision-making process at first. As we stepped a little further into my cancer journey and started to see our way forward, we realized that maybe she could still do it all, with a little help from our family and friends. I am so happy and relieved that she postponed that initial decision to close her practice long enough to realize that it was something that didn't need to be done. The thought of losing it after all the hard work she had put into creating and growing it, all because of my illness, is something I'm not sure I could have gotten over.

By the fall of 2021, her practice was thriving. What had started as just her performing in-home and telehealth visits had grown to a team of four employees (Katie plus another nurse practitioner and two office staff) and a full office. They had a full slate of patients in the office, many homebound patients who they went to see, and patients at assisted living and senior care facilities. She and her team were offering care to a segment of the population that was unable to get to a doctor's office to be cared for. Her practice was doing exactly what she'd always hoped: offering patient-focused care to the people who really needed it.

But then misfortune struck. On October 15, 2021, Katie's office building was demolished. Shortly after midnight, a driver for a logistics company fell asleep at the wheel, drove his semi-truck off the road, and smashed it through the side of Katie's office building at fifty miles an hour. Fortunately, the driver was able to walk away from the accident with no significant injuries. The building, on the other hand, was left in a state of complete disaster.

When we woke up that morning, I saw that I had missed a text in the middle of the night from a friend of mine who worked for our local fire department. It simply read, "Are you awake?" I replied to him as soon as I read it, asking if everything was all right. He replied with a picture of Katie's office building with the last six feet of that semi-truck sticking out of the side of it. The rest of the truck was buried deep inside the building.

Katie and I were in shock. It was the most surreal feeling ever. This was impossibly bad luck. Maybe even less probable than a forty-seven-year-old healthy man being diagnosed with pancreatic cancer. This couldn't be happening to us. How bad can one family's luck be?

Much later that day, after the first responders were finally able to remove the semi from the side of the building, we were able to get a peek inside through the front window. It was even worse than we could have imagined. Katie's desk, which was just inside the wall that he drove through, was completely disintegrated. It was like it never existed; not a splinter of it remained. All the walls between her exam rooms, lab, and office were completely smashed. The ceiling and roof had collapsed in places. It was a complete loss. All her equipment, all her furniture, everything was completely gone. We knew that it was going to be a long rebuild, and she wouldn't be seeing patients in the office again anytime soon.

As with most things, I tried my hardest to find the positive in difficult situations. In this case, there was definitely one huge and obvious positive: The accident had happened in the middle of the night, when no one was there. If it had been during the workday, and Katie had been at her desk, she would most definitely have been killed. If patients had been in the exam rooms, there likely would have been multiple casualties, or at a minimum many severe injuries. The building and possessions inside were replaceable, but Katie and her patients were definitely not.

Just over one year after Katie had to consider closing the doors of her practice because of my cancer diagnosis, she once again had to think about shutting it down due to the damages caused by the semi-truck accident. Insurance would cover the loss of the office property, but we had very real concerns that the loss of income from not being able to see patients in the office might be enough to mean it would make more sense to just close it. The preliminary estimates were that the rebuild would take a minimum of six months. That's a very long time to not be able to see patients.

But Katie doesn't give up easily. Like me, she's a fighter. After the initial shock and a lot of tears from both of us, she decided to figure out how to keep things going until the office could be rebuilt. And she did figure it out. She figured out how to manage all the insurance red tape and the complicated legal situation, and she figured out how to continue to see her patients as best as possible until she had her office back up and running.

She pivoted back to where she'd started, seeing patients via telehealth and home visits. They also continued to see homebound patients and patients at assisted living and senior care facilities and grew that part of the business even more. After a few months, she was able to convert a conference room in the office building that wasn't damaged into a makeshift exam room, allowing her to see some patients in the office again.

Being the incredibly smart businessperson that she is (but rarely gives herself credit for), she had figured out how to keep her business operating and thriving despite that incredibly unlucky accident that had the potential to destroy everything she had created. She refused to let it fail. Per usual, she overcame the adversity that was handed to her and turned it into success.

When someone in a family is hit with adversity, it hits everyone else in the family right along with them. My cancer had obviously hammered Katie and the kids just as hard, or maybe harder, than it had hit me. Without knowing it, Katie was once again showing me the path to overcoming adversity by how she dealt with the semi accident. Our entire family would soon need to lean into that precedent of perseverance and pull together even tighter as a family. As difficult as the semi-truck accident was, it was nothing compared to what our family and community would face next.

CHAPTER 18

THE WORST DAY OF MY CANCER BATTLE

For most people, imagining how I felt on the day I was diagnosed is next to impossible. On a scale of one to shit, that day was about as shitty as it gets. So, it seems like that should've been the low point for me, the worst of all the bad days. But then November 30, 2021, came along. On the list of really bad days, that day suddenly ranked right up there with, or even surpassed, my diagnosis day.

The day started normally. Landon headed off to high school, Parker to middle school, and Grady headed to elementary school. I was on my break from workouts and treatments due to my severe hand-foot syndrome but was almost fully recovered after the multi-week break.

I was working from my home office that day, but instead of my typical empty house with just the two dogs and myself, I had two added officemates. Katie was also working from home, since her office was closed due to the semi accident, and Tristen was also at home studying, spending the day on his laptop at the dining room table.

In the early afternoon, the day took an awful turn. From my office, I heard Katie say, "Oh, shit." All the parents of Landon's friend group had a group text, and one of the moms had sent an alert. "I don't want to cause any panic, but please text each of your boys. Gabe just texted from school, and they're in lockdown, supposedly for an active shooting. This does not appear to be a drill!"

I stood next to Katie as she read it aloud and felt the worst sense of fear and panic start to overtake me. Katie immediately texted Landon. No response. I texted him. No response. We waited a few minutes, then texted again. No response. The group text was continuing at the same time. One by one, each set of parents replied that they had made contact with their son and they were all locked down in their classrooms, barricaded behind doors, not fully sure of how bad things were out in those halls, but safe for the moment.

But we had still not received a reply from Landon. The sense of panic was greater than I can ever remember, even worse than that day just over a year earlier when I had learned I had cancer. It was unbearable. Finally, after approximately twenty minutes of no contact, Katie called him. He answered. He whispered, "I'm OK, Mom. But I can't talk. I'm building a wall of chairs in my classroom that we're hiding behind. I'm OK though. I love you." And with that he hung up. By this point Katie and I were sobbing in fear.

In our panic, I hadn't really noticed Tristen quietly sitting in the adjacent dining room. He was watching it all transpire. After that brief call with Landon, I finally noticed that Tristan, too, was sobbing uncontrollably. We grabbed him in a huge hug and pulled him into the living room with us. The three of us sat on the couch, silent except for our crying, deep in fearful thoughts, waiting for Landon to call back.

While waiting, Katie texted with Parker, who was in her middle school a mile or so away from the high school. They too were in lockdown, but safe. Parker was learning about what was happening just up the road at the high school in real time via texts from friends and social media while she sat in her classroom in lockdown. It was so surreal for us as we watched this horror unfold. We had to assure her repeatedly via text that Landon was OK, which we were praying was still the case. She was obviously scared beyond belief as well.

We would learn afterward that Grady was also in lockdown in his elementary classroom, approximately five miles away from the high school. Without a phone, he was mostly unaware of the seriousness of what was occurring at his older brother's school. I'm thankful for that at least.

After what seemed like hours but was actually only around fifteen or twenty minutes, Landon called to tell us the lockdown was over and they were releasing all the students from the school. We were to pick him up at our local grocery store parking lot, which was just a few hundred yards down the road from the high school.

Katie, Tristen, and I frantically jumped in my truck and sped off. I cannot adequately describe the scene there. It was mind-blowing. There were four or five news and police helicopters flying low over the school and the grocery store. It felt like something out of a video game or action movie. Thousands of parents were on foot in the parking lot, searching desperately for their children. Thousands of kids were frantically coming down the hill en masse from the high school to that parking lot. Everyone was crying. Everyone was terrified. At that point, we only knew that an actual school shooting had occurred, with some injuries at a minimum, but no one knew who was injured or how severely.

As we anxiously waited for Landon to come down that hill, my cousin Audrey's daughter Norah, who was also a junior in the high school, emerged from the crowd of students in front of me. We locked eyes and immediately burst into tears. I grabbed her tightly and held her in a hug. She would not let go. I could not let go—I just held her. I will never forget the look in that sweet girl's eyes. She should have never had to experience that level of fear. No one should.

Audrey is a teacher in a different school district close to an hour away. She was speeding as fast as traffic would allow to get there. Thankfully Norah had found us in the meantime, and we kept her close with us until Audrey arrived.

Shortly after that, Landon appeared on that hill. We all grabbed him and held him in a big group hug, not wanting to let go. Not ever wanting to let go. He stated repeatedly that he was OK. He told us he had to go with his best friend Jacob to find Jacob's little brother Max, who was a freshman. Max has Down syndrome, and they didn't know if he and his classmates had made it down to the parking lot. The two of them ran off looking for Max.

As we were waiting for Landon to return, we talked with many of the parents we knew. Those we talked with had all found their kids. But we talked of a few of the kids that we knew who were not accounted for yet. The fear of the unspeakable began to creep into our minds.

After Landon had returned (they had found Max, thankfully), Katie, Tristen, Landon, and I climbed into my truck and drove away from the chaos, all still in shock. After getting Landon home, we drove to the middle school and elementary school to get the two younger ones and get them home safely under our roof and under our careful watch. That terrifying day was close to being over, but the struggle and horrible aftermath for our entire community was just beginning.

So our family of six was home safely. But what the hell do you do next in a situation like that? We were obviously worried about Landon, who had just experienced the inconceivable, but he just kept saying he was OK. He went to his room as soon as we were home. Katie and I turned the news on to try to put our arms around the severity of the situation while repeatedly going in to check on him.

It hit me hard when I saw President Biden come on the national news to give his thoughts and prayers to our students and community. Our students and community. How was this possible? How was the president of the United States talking about our little southeastern Michigan community and the tragedy we were enduring? This was the type of event we all knew unfortunately occurred far too often in our country, but it wasn't supposed to ever happen to us specifically. Oxford was now tied to the communities of Columbine, Sandy Hook, Parkland, and way too many others that have endured the horror of a school shooting.

The horrible emotions I was experiencing were reminiscent of those I had felt just thirteen months prior when I'd called my parents to tell them that I'd been diagnosed with pancreatic cancer. I had watched as they struggled to cope with the idea of potentially losing one of their children. Now here I was, struggling with the same thoughts.

We still didn't know who the monster was who had done this, who was injured, and who, if anyone, was dead. The news was slow on details at first. We started getting more information via the many texts that we were exchanging with neighbors and friends. We learned of a few who were injured. And then we got the worst news possible: three Oxford High School students did not survive, and a fourth was lost within a day. Seven others had been shot and injured, including one teacher.

Through texts, we got the first name of one of our angels: Tate Myre. Tate was known by all in the community. He was the best athlete, friends with pretty much everyone, and just an overall amazing human being. Katie and I were in the living room when we learned that Tate didn't survive that day. We again started crying as we tried to understand how this could happen to such an amazing kid from such an amazing family. It just wasn't fair.

As we talked, we didn't notice Landon had come out of his bedroom. He overheard our discussion, which is how he learned of the loss of his friend Tate. He turned completely white. Contrary to his claims, he was not all right prior to learning this, but he was definitely not all right after. It hit him hard. I think that made it far too real for him.

The bad news continued to come out as the evening progressed. We learned of the tragically lost lives: Tate Myre, Madisyn Baldwin, Hana St. Juliana, and Justin Shilling. They were taken far too soon by this horrific and senseless tragedy. We also learned of the other seven who were injured and hospitalized. Four lost, seven more injured, and an entire community changed forever.

The news eventually reported the name of the shooter. He was a fifteen-year-old sophomore. I asked Landon if he knew him. He said he did not, but then he saw the boy's face on the TV and did know who he was. He had actually been in Landon's fifth-hour class, although they'd never talked. That was the class Landon was in when the lockdown started and the shootings occurred. Landon realized that if the shooter had decided to go to his own class before starting his evil rampage instead of going to a bathroom, things could have been much, much worse for Landon and our family.

This only made the horrible situation hit even harder. Landon started to have survivor's guilt. The struggles that young man endured due to this event, in conjunction with the struggles of watching his father fight cancer, will be something he has to carry and manage for his entire life. He is resilient, but the effects of living through something like that do not go away easily, if ever.

Our community was challenged with grief that few in this world can understand. In mid-December, we had a vigil in our quaint little downtown. It was an event organized to help our community grieve and attempt to take a small step past the tragedy together. Unfortunately, a teenager became overwhelmed and passed out. This caused some panic and people started yelling "gun," running frantically away from the stage. The whole crowd went into a frenzy. What was supposed to be an event to help our community's healing had suddenly turned into more terror and fear. The emotional wounds that were still fresh from November 30 were torn wide open again.

We then had the funerals. Multiple funerals for teenagers are something no one should ever have to experience; it's just too much for the heart to handle. We attended Tate's and Hana's funerals, both beautiful tributes to two beautiful souls, but still so, so hard to accept.

Finding a positive here was impossible at first. But some did come out of it. At restaurants in town, I started to notice everyone hugging when they saw each other. Handshakes became a thing of the past. After such a horrible experience, only a hug seemed right. People were nicer to each other, more supportive. We had experienced something that no one ever should, and through that horrific event, we were bonded together. It's sad that it takes something so bad for a change like this to happen.

Additionally, some incredible organizations were formed because of that day; 42 Strong is the nonprofit started by the Myre family in honor of Tate. Tate's football number was 42. If things had gone differently, the way they should have, you would have eventually seen him on TV wearing that 42 for a college team somewhere. I like to think it would have been my alma mater, Michigan State. He was that good. But he never got that chance, unfortunately.

The Myre family started 42 Strong within months of November 30. The speed and amount of detail with which they acted still blows my mind. What they have created is second to none, and they did it almost immediately and flawlessly. 42 Strong is a peer-to-peer mentoring program through which high school students mentor younger students in an effort to ensure kids have the necessary support needed in those difficult school-age years and don't fall through the cracks and take a negative turn, similar to the Oxford shooter. The goal is to give kids a resource that can help to prevent future tragedies. You can learn more about it and donate (42strong-tate.org).

I would give anything to erase November 30, 2021, from history, make it so it never happened. But that unfortunately cannot happen. So, we try to move on, while also never forgetting and always honoring those who were lost. We try to become better people. We try to continue to be a better community. We try to be there for all the kids growing up in this community. We try to grow. Because that's all you can do.

CHAPTER 19

SO YOU'RE SAYING THERE'S A CHANCE . . .

After the tragedy of the shooting, it was a little difficult to focus on staying positive and fighting cancer again. Even something as serious as pancreatic cancer seemed unimportant in the wake of that horrific event. But as time went on and our community began to adapt and adjust, I shifted my focus back.

I had a CT scan followed by an MRI in December to check the status of the tumor and check for any spread. The results we received from those scans were nothing short of miraculous. The radiology reports from both scans read, "No Evidence of Disease." No evidence of disease, also known as NED in the cancer world, is the report we all hope and pray to get someday. It doesn't necessarily mean we're cancer-free, but it means the cancer has been reduced enough that it is not evident in the scans. This was huge news.

When I met with my radiation oncologist, he was almost in shock. He said, "Man, I was really glad I was sitting down when I reviewed the images. I couldn't believe it! There's nothing there."

He then reminded me that just because the cancer wasn't visible on the images anymore, didn't mean it was gone. It was more like it had shrunk significantly and was now just kind of hiding. Regardless, it was the best report I'd received since I was originally diagnosed.

I firmly believed it was a miracle from God. I knew that God had chosen to do what couldn't be done via the attempted Whipple procedure and had removed my tumor Himself. To be at a NED status just over a year after being diagnosed with pancreatic cancer without surgical intervention was basically unheard of. God had blessed us with a miracle.

With that said, I knew I had to keep fighting, as it could come back, grow, or spread to other organs at any time. I knew cancer was a sneaky and scary adversary, so I wasn't about to let up and allow it to catch me off guard. As we started 2022, I continued my maintenance chemotherapy plan, worked out as regularly as possible, and stayed positive.

•   •   •

I tried to stay active and busy in as many ways as possible. In late January, I started snowboarding after a few years off, because it was something I wasn't "supposed" to be able to do. I had pancreatic cancer, I was going through pretty intense chemotherapy, and I was pushing fifty years old. Most people wouldn't pair those things up with snowboarding. In my mind, that just meant I had all the more reason to go for it!

After a few rides on our local hills alone and with Landon in early January, I scheduled a two-day trip up north with two of my best friends from high school, Alistair and Josh. It had been quite a few years since the three of us had been together. But we fell right back in step, just like always. These two were more brothers than friends.

The night before hitting the slopes, we hung out at Josh's cabin near the ski resort, drinking some bourbons and beers, sharing many old stories, and laughing until it hurt. I was back in my element, with the best of friends, completely at peace, full of joy, and just ecstatic to be there.

There's just something about being around people that you can share anything with. Those rare people who don't require you to put up walls or worry about saying the wrong thing. It's with those people that you can share your darkest moments and find your greatest joys. With those two, the cancer didn't matter. I could talk about it with them, but it wasn't what defined me. For those few days, it was like I was transported back to a simpler time before the cancer had taken over my world, a time when only fun and laughter mattered.

The next morning, we realized that we weren't as young as we once were. All three of us were hurting from a little too much fun and a little too much bourbon. It was a harsh reminder that hangovers are significantly worse at fifty than they are in your twenties. The recovery was much slower than it had once been.

But we'd gotten back together that weekend to snowboard, and that's exactly what we did. We made it to the resort for the first chairlift despite the slight pounding in our heads. It was bitterly cold that day. One of the side effects of the chemo I was on was severe numbness in the hands and feet when cold. The weather that day qualified as beyond cold, with temperatures around zero degrees Fahrenheit. That wasn't going to stop me—not when I had the rare opportunity to do one of my favorite things with some of my favorite people. I was snowboarding. I was with my boys. I was alive! And I was living my best life possible in that moment.

It was as if all those positives drowned out the numbness in my hands and feet, making it possible to just ride and laugh with Al and Josh. I clearly remember each moment of that day on the slopes feeling like it was in slow motion. When the sun poked through a little, it felt brighter, more intense. The smell of the fresh, frigid air seemed fresher than I could ever remember. Each turn I made on each run was in slow motion, allowing me to feel as if my board, the hill, and I were one connected thing. It was beautiful.

•   •   •

In late March, I had my quarterly MRI to assess my cancer status. Amazingly, the radiology report again read "No Evidence of Disease." While I planned to continue the maintenance chemo for the foreseeable future, I felt it was time to investigate the potential of trying the Whipple procedure again, which was the only potential "cure" for pancreatic cancer. I wanted to be cured. My status was very good at that time, but the cancer was still in there somewhere, and I wanted it out. My oncology team agreed that investigating options for a second surgical attempt was the correct next step.

My previous surgeon had stated unequivocally that he would never attempt a Whipple on me again. He said that it couldn't be done successfully and shouldn't be attempted, by him or anyone else. I had refused to accept his assessment at the time and accepted it even less after that MRI in March 2022. I didn't agree with definitive negative statements. I was determined to never give up. And that means never saying never. I decided that I needed to advocate for my own healthcare plan and take it upon myself to find a different surgeon who would be willing to give the surgery another attempt.

I started searching online for specialists in the Whipple procedure. Due to the high risk and complexity of that procedure, there are very few to choose from. To ensure my insurance would cover this extremely high-cost surgery, I knew it was best to use an in-state surgeon. So, my search was fairly limited. At the time, there were probably fewer than ten surgeons in the entire state of Michigan who were considered experts in the Whipple procedure.

Fairly quickly in my search, I found Dr. K, a surgeon at another metro-Detroit cancer center. Something deep in my heart told me that he was my guy. I can't explain it, but I knew. I truly believe that God led me to Dr. K.

Even with the certainty I had in my heart, I did my due diligence and research to ensure I was correct. I followed up with my previous oncologist, Dr. A, who in late 2021 had left her former cancer institute and moved to the one where Dr. K was. She confirmed that Dr. K was an amazing surgeon and someone I should contact about a second surgical attempt. I also reached out to an acquaintance who ran a local cancer support nonprofit organization that I was involved with. She also strongly recommended Dr. K, who was on their board of directors. The opinion of those two meant a lot to me and adequately confirmed my feelings that he was the surgeon I should pursue. I scheduled an initial consultation with Dr. K.

Prior to my consultation, we had a spring break trip planned for Florida in the last week of March with Landon, his friends, and his friends' parents. After the horrific event Landon and his friends had endured on November 30, we wanted to give them all a great spring break together. We rented a large house in the Florida panhandle and enjoyed the sun, the pool, and the gulf. I was able to complete some amazing outdoor runs in the sun while there, taking full advantage of the week away from our Michigan winter.

On that trip, I also had a life-changing experience of a different kind. While sitting by the pool one day, I received a message from an old friend from high school who still lived in Muskegon, where I had grown up. While we were no longer in regular contact with each other, he had been following my cancer journey closely on Facebook. He had a friend from work who had just been diagnosed with pancreatic cancer and wanted to know if I would be willing to talk to this friend, as he was really struggling with the situation. I of course agreed.

The gentleman gave me a call later that evening. I spent close to an hour on the phone with him. I told him my story. I told him how I was fighting. I shared the strategy and methods I had been using to cope and to fight the cancer. I told him a pancreatic cancer diagnosis didn't have to be an immediate death sentence. Mostly, I just listened to his concerns and fears and tried to be as supportive and inspiring as possible.

The friend who had connected us told me our talk had really helped this gentleman. I was able to give him a little hope and provide some inspiration. It felt really good to give back a little to someone facing similar struggles. So many had helped me through my fight, and it was so nice to be the one giving the support versus just receiving it. I needed to find as many ways and as many people as possible to inspire and help. That one phone call, with a gentleman I had never met, significantly changed my goals in life. After that, I knew for certain, down to my core, that God was giving me additional time on this earth to make a difference. I needed to use whatever time I had to give back to others, like so many had done for me.

As my initial consultation with Dr. K approached, I had one small concern. My scans in December and March showed no evidence of disease, which was good news overall, but for a surgical consult it could cause a slight problem. If the tumor wasn't on the scans, what was the surgeon supposed to consult? How was he supposed to evaluate if he could remove it? How could he adequately assess if it was still engaged with the artery? With no evidence of the tumor, would Dr. K be willing or able to evaluate whether he could perform the surgery at all?

Prior to the consultation, Dr. K wanted a CT scan performed at his hospital. The methodology and technique for CT scans is apparently slightly different between hospital systems. Dr. K wanted to see a scan done the way he was accustomed to and had helped develop for his own cancer center.

That new scan quickly alleviated my concern of the tumor not being evident. It did show the tumor, at a size of approximately 1.5 cm in diameter. It was still there, but apparently not active enough to show up on the other hospital systems' scans. The next very important question was whether Dr. K felt there were adequate margins to attempt to remove it via surgery. This was a more difficult question. Determining margins at the detailed level that was required was not possible with the accuracy and granularity provided in the scan. So, Dr. K was going to have to trust his gut.

At my initial consultation, my intuition that Dr. K was the right surgeon for me was further confirmed. He immediately gave me a comfortable feeling. He had a positive demeanor, was very professional in our discussions, and overall just gave off a great vibe. He was also dressed very impressively, in an awesome tailored suit with an extraordinary bow tie. I liked his style! His image screamed professionalism and confidence, both things I considered very important in a person who would be doing a major surgery on me.

After evaluating the images, Dr. K led with the good news: He was willing to attempt a second Whipple procedure on me. There were some caveats, though. He wanted to ensure I fully understood all the risks before deciding to proceed. The second surgical attempt would not be easy and came with a relatively low probability of success and potentially life-threatening dangers.

Following the initial Whipple attempt, my previous surgeon had used staples while closing me back up. The healing around those staples had produced significant scar tissue. My radiation treatments had also left substantial scar tissue throughout my abdominal area, making a second attempt much more difficult and higher risk than the first surgery, which was already pretty high risk.

To quote Dr. K: "All of that scar tissue is like cement, meaning I'll have to chisel where I would prefer to be making precise, delicate cuts." Trust me, "chisel" is not the word you want used when someone is talking about cutting through your abdomen and internal organs.

The increased complexity for an already complex surgery meant the surgery would likely take twelve to fifteen hours to complete, with only about a 50 percent chance of success. There was also an added risk of serious complications occurring during the surgery, and things going very bad. Very bad in this case meant I likely wouldn't live.

I had a very difficult decision to make. I could continue on with maintenance and hope the tumor remained dormant, but this couldn't continue to be successful forever. The other option was subjecting myself to an extremely high-risk surgery that had just a 50 percent chance of being successful.

Even if the surgery was successful, there was still a strong likelihood the cancer could eventually return and spread. I definitely needed some time to think and pray on this critical decision. I knew whatever I decided would be the biggest decision of my cancer journey and probably the biggest decision of my entire life.

• • •

As spring came to a close, I still hadn't decided whether to proceed with the second surgery attempt. But as we approached Memorial Day, the correct decision suddenly became very clear to me.

I had prayed on it a lot, and on the morning of May 24, I told Katie that I was 100 percent sure what I wanted to do. Although the surgery was very high risk and had a relatively low chance for success, I was absolutely certain that I couldn't pass up the chance to improve my odds of getting rid of the cancer and extending my amazing life. It was far from a sure thing that the surgery would give me that, but the odds of extended life with surgery were better than without surgery.

I called Dr. K. The earliest we could schedule it was late July. My birthday is August 1, and I wanted to wait to ensure I had that forty-ninth birthday, just in case. We decided to delay until

September 23, after the summer and Labor Day. Obviously, there was a fair chance that things could change with my status in those four months, but we had a date on the calendar at last. I was getting my second chance, the one I had hoped for and prayed about for so long.

CHAPTER 20

PREPARING FOR WHIPPLE ATTEMPT #2

With that crucial decision made, I set out to enjoy my summer to its fullest. I was still on my maintenance chemo plan and doing fairly well with it. We again spent plenty of time at the lake. I was even able to get away for a weekend for some golf and fun with my college roommates.

In early July, Katie and I decided it would be good to get away, just the two of us, for a long weekend in one of our favorite Michigan cities, Traverse City. We typically tried to get there at least once or twice a year, and always absolutely loved it. This trip seemed even a little more special for some reason. We toured the wineries, enjoyed some shopping, ate some amazing meals, and toured some little nearby cities we hadn't been to before. It was an incredible, relaxing long weekend away with the love of my life. With my pending surgery, I absorbed and appreciated every minute of it even more than usual.

That trip also firmly cemented my decision to go ahead with the second surgery. All I could think of that whole weekend was how lucky I was. How lucky I was to be married to her. How lucky I was to have four incredible kids with her. How lucky I was to live the life I had. I wanted, and needed, to ensure I was doing absolutely everything in my power to continue living my amazing life for as long as possible. The upcoming surgery gave me the best chance at doing that.

In late July, Dr. K scheduled one last CT scan for me to ensure there was no spread of the cancer and we were OK to continue with the surgery in September. As always, awaiting scan results is extremely stressful. It actually has its own term: scanxiety. Fortunately, this result was once again a positive one, showing no growth or spread.

After we discussed those positive results, Dr. K's nurse handed me my pre-op preparation packet. For some reason, taking that packet of instructions into my hand hit me very hard. The reality of my opportunity hit me like a ton of bricks. All of the uncertainty and struggles I had endured leading up to that moment had finally brought me to this critical juncture. The odds of someone with pancreatic cancer getting the opportunity to have one Whipple procedure are only 20 percent. I was getting chance number two! I was a complete anomaly. This chance was a miracle.

As the enormity of that hit me while I grabbed that packet, I suddenly burst into tears. The sweet nurses hugged me and tried to comfort me. To be honest, it was all just so overwhelming. I knew the chances for success were only 50 percent. But 50 percent was better than 0 percent. I had a chance. And with that, it was time to go home and start pre-fight training-camp version two.

• • •

I spent a large portion of the rest of my summer and early fall coaching Grady in football. We had an awesome team of around twenty-five fourth-, fifth-, and sixth-graders. The coaching staff, all dads of the players, became amazing, supportive friends as we went through the preseason practices and preparations. With practices five nights a week, coaching gave me a much-needed distraction from thinking about the risks of my pending surgery. I was able to focus on teaching the boys the game of football and ensuring we were all having a lot of fun while doing it.

The inspiration I received from the boys on that team was equally amazing. Their consistent hard work and preparation for their upcoming games was awesome to be a part of. They inspired me to work hard and prepare for my next big game: the surgery. When I was struggling to get out for a run, I thought of them. I thought of my fellow coaches who were so supportive of me. And that was enough to get me out on the road running, working hard, preparing. Coaching that Oxford Junior Wildcat football team right up until the day before my surgery helped me so much in preparation for that big day.

$$\bullet \quad \bullet \quad \bullet$$

Regardless of the sport, coaching my kids' sports teams while I went through cancer became a big part of my support system. As much as I loved playing sports, I loved coaching them even more. It was so enjoyable seeing kids grow to love the sports that I did, and playing a small part in that happening through coaching was an awesome experience. At the start, I wasn't sure I'd be able to keep coaching after I was diagnosed, but as I started to feel a little better it seemed like something that could really help distract me. So, I decided that I would push the cancer aside and coach. No excuses.

I first coached Grady in lacrosse. Grady was the first to play lacrosse in our family. He picked it up quickly and loved it. It became his favorite sport and one of mine as well. His first year, they needed a coach for his local team, so I happily volunteered. It gave me something else to focus on, and it allowed me to be outside, in the fresh air, with some amazing young athletes who inspired me daily.

Lacrosse is originally a Native American game. The Native Americans called it the "medicine game." To them, it was more of a spiritual ceremony than sport. They believed that the game would help heal the sick members of their tribe. I believe it did just that for me. As people in the lacrosse community found out about my cancer, the support I received was incredible. All the other coaches in our program were super supportive and became great friends. The parents of my team were awesome, supporting me through it all. The team I coached, Grady included, inspired me with their play and fight throughout the entire season. I wasn't sure about coaching lacrosse at first, but deciding to do it ended up being one of the best decisions I could have made.

I also received support from kids I had coached years prior, alongside Tristen and Landon. Those kids were all away in college or in high school when they learned that I had cancer. I received so many texts from them, checking on me and offering support. Many were kids I hadn't seen or coached in four or five years, yet they still contacted me and stayed in touch as I went through my battle.

A few who were playing high school sports at the time did things to honor me in my fight. Some wrote my initials on the tape they used on their wrists for football and lacrosse games. Another wore my name on his special jersey for a cancer fundraiser Game for a Cure football game. The support I received from these former players meant so much to me and made me realize that I also must have had a positive impact on their lives for them to give back so much to me.

Cancer made me realize just how important coaching was to me. Even while being sick, it was something I loved and needed to do. Coaching has become one of my biggest passions. It's something that I'm good at. It's something that I love. And it's something that I can do to give back to my community.

I'm not sure I would have realized how important it was for me if I wasn't doing it while also fighting my biggest fight. Coaching allowed me to give back a little to our local athletic community, but the support I received in return as I battled cancer was so much more than I could have ever given. It was another amazing ripple effect. I gave a little through coaching; the players, other coaches, and the parents gave me support in return that was a hundredfold.

Cancer is one hell of an opponent. The more people you can have on your team supporting you in the fight, the better.

· · ·

Like the earlier surgical attempt, I prepared as if I were getting ready for a championship-level boxing match. I wanted to ensure I was ready—physically, mentally, emotionally, and spiritually—by September 23.

Approximately seven weeks prior to the surgery date, I stopped my maintenance chemo plan. I needed that amount of time without the chemo to let it flush out of my system, allowing my body to recover and strengthen before it went through the extreme stress of the second Whipple attempt. Being off the chemotherapy allowed me to train hard. My body felt so much better once I stopped taking it, making my workouts and daily activities so much more enjoyable.

I continued to run multiple times a week in the months leading up to surgery. My body was getting stronger, and I felt more and more ready. On one of those runs in early September, I started thinking about my pending surgery, and the severity of it almost stopped me in my tracks. For the first time in a very long time, I was overcome with fear. My mind filled with all the things that could go wrong, to the point I could barely breathe. I felt like I was on mile twenty, when in reality I was only around one mile in.

But I somehow pushed through. The run slowly cleared my mind. Finally, a few miles in, those three little words that had carried me through so much popped back into my head very clearly:

"*faith* over fear." As quickly as the fear had come, it was gone. I was breathing fine again and just running, suddenly at complete peace. I was ready.

On another training run around that time, my mind shifted to the bigger picture. I focused on what I was fighting for, beyond just preparing for surgery. The word "legacy" filled my head. I realized that I was fighting to leave a legacy with whatever time I had left on this earth. I wasn't just running and trying to change myself to prepare for the surgery; I was in a frantic race to become the best version of myself for the longer term.

All the work I was putting in to fight cancer was also enabling me to become a better version of myself in general. It was giving me a chance to leave a legacy that my wife and kids and family and friends would be proud of. I realized my fight was bigger than just the cancer. My fight was to be better, in general. My fight was enabling me to leave a legacy of being a good husband, a good father, a good friend, and a person who did everything in his power to help others.

In the last few days before the surgery, I wrapped up my pre-fight training-camp mode. I was ready. My body was prepared. My mind was prepared. I was at peace. I had extreme hope. I took those last few days to rest up and enjoy some time with family and friends, as I was likely looking at around three weeks away from everyone while stuck in the hospital.

Two nights before the surgery date, Katie and I went to dinner with our closest friends for a big night out. The Whipple procedure was a high-risk surgery with a really long recovery time, and the surgical prep paperwork stated I needed to be on a clear liquid diet for twelve hours prior to my surgery, so this was likely going to be the last good meal I was able to eat for ages. I loaded up on a mouthwatering steak and lobster dinner. It was the perfect finale of life with cancer—or so I thought.

That amazing dinner almost caused a delay in the surgery timing. The next morning, I received my pre-surgery check-in call from one of the nurses. She asked if I was on clear liquids already. Confused, I told her I still had a few hours before that was supposed to begin. There was apparently a misunderstanding, as I was supposed to be on clear liquids diet for thirty-six hours before surgery, not just the twelve that my paperwork had shown.

Based on the time of day I learned of this, I was going to be on the clear-liquid diet for only eighteen hours instead of the required thirty-six. And that steak and lobster dinner I had so thoroughly enjoyed was the furthest thing from a clear liquid! I had a brief moment of panic, but the nurse reassured me that it would likely be fine. She let me go so she could contact Dr. K to determine what I should do next. She told me to just relax and be patient. That was easier said than done.

She called back. Dr. K determined that we would proceed as planned with the surgery, regardless of me only being on the clear liquid diet for my shortened eighteen-hour timeframe. Thankfully the misunderstanding hadn't been a more significant issue. A delay in surgery would have been so difficult to accept. Fortunately, that wasn't necessary.

We were now fully on schedule. We were less than twenty-four hours away from the opportunity I had been waiting and praying for. It was time for my miracle chance, a statistically improbable second chance, at getting rid of my tumor! It was go time.

CHAPTER 21

MY MIRACLE SURGERY

The night before the surgery, Katie and I stayed at the on-site apartments at the hospital. Katie would be staying there for a week or two while I recovered, to stay close and support me.

The expectation was that the surgery would take twelve to fifteen hours, and that I would need to be in the hospital for approximately twenty days to recover. This surgery was major. Fortunately for me, my role in the process was pretty simple. I basically just had to take a twelve- to fifteen-hour nap, while Dr. K did all the hard work. I had done everything within my power to prepare. It was now in the hands of God and Dr. K.

That night before the surgery was relatively uneventful. I spent a lot of time praying before going to bed and was surprisingly very much at peace and very relaxed. Despite the severity of the surgery and the low likelihood of success, I was very confident. My faith was strong, and I was fully leaning into it.

I woke up feeling great. I showered, following the pre-surgical instructions to ensure I was properly cleaned up, got dressed, made a quick Facebook post asking for a few prayers, and then sat down to pray one last time with Katie.

Exactly two years and one day after my diagnosis with pancreatic cancer, I was checked in and being prepared for my second chance at surgically removing the tumor from my body. Just like the previous surgical attempt, I was very positive and upbeat in pre-op. I joked with my nurses and the anesthesiology team. I was not tense or nervous at all. I had prepared so hard for this opportunity. I truly felt that I had done everything possible to be as ready as possible. I also had complete faith in Dr. K's capabilities and in God's plan for me. My faith had completely pushed aside any fear or nervousness.

The nurses started my IV and began running fluids into my system. The anesthesiology team gave me an epidural to help with the significant pain that would be coming postsurgery. Finally, with all the pre-op checks complete, I gave Katie a big hug and kiss goodbye and was wheeled toward the operating room.

Once in the OR, they moved me to the operating table, and I asked the surgical team to join me in prayer. They obliged and we prayed together. After we completed that quick prayer, the anesthesiologist placed the mask on my face, and I was out.

For me, it was all over in what felt like an instant. That was definitely not the case for Dr. K and his team. When I awoke in the post-op recovery room, Katie was standing by with some of the nurses. I was of course still very groggy. But as soon as I awoke, I instantly asked if Dr. K had been able to remove the tumor. The answer Katie and the nurses gave me was a miraculous "Yes!" My brain apparently couldn't fully comprehend that answer yet, because I kept asking the same question probably ten to twenty times. Every time the answer was the same glorious response of "Yes!" I had been given the answer I had prayed for so many times.

The surgery had taken approximately thirteen-and-a-half hours. That's a very long time to be under anesthesia. I was groggy and a little slow mentally for almost two days after. But once I was able to better comprehend things and have a somewhat coherent conversation, Katie gave me more details about the actual surgery. She told me that Dr. K looked like he had just completed a marathon when he finally came out to give her the update. He was sweaty and looked absolutely exhausted. Once he had opened me up, he found that things were even more complicated than he originally expected. The scar tissue was even more severe than he had predicted. Once he was able to chisel and work his way through that, he found the tumor was still significantly engaged with the superior mesenteric artery. But miraculously, none of that had stopped him.

My recovery process was not an easy one, given that it was about as serious of a surgery as I could have endured. The first few days after were really rough. The epidural and pain pump kept my pain relatively under control, at least. I slept a lot over those first few days. It felt like I slept more than I was awake. I also had some very frustrating mental battles. In my somewhat confused state, I was convinced that there was something wrong that they weren't telling me. At times, I was convinced that the tumor was still in there, and they were lying to me because I was really about to die. I even had instances where I was sure I was already dead, and I was seeing myself in the hospital bed from above. These thoughts were extremely vivid and extraordinarily scary. It was torturous.

As the drugs finally flushed completely out of my system, my mind started to recover, and I started to feel like myself again. At that point, I knew I was going to be OK, and I set out to go full speed into the recovery process. Just like after the prior attempted Whipple procedure, I knew that getting my body moving would be the key to kickstarting the recovery process. It had worked to speed up my exit from the hospital the last time, and my plan was that I could again shorten my stay well under the expected twenty days.

As I said, those first few days consisted mostly of sleep. But when I was awake, I forced myself to go for walks. Katie facilitated that as well. She spent the entirety of those days by my bedside, even though I was mostly just sleeping. When I woke up, she would tell me it was time to walk. She pushed me as much as, or more than, I pushed myself.

The walks were very short at first. But each time, I made sure I went just a little further than the previous walk, even if it was only one step further. It was painful and difficult, but over my time battling cancer I had learned that I was pretty good at doing hard things. So I walked, despite the pain and the struggle. I pushed a little further down that hall each time. By the third day, I was able to walk a lap around the entire floor. Shortly after that lap, it was multiple laps, multiple times a day. I was on my way to recovery, and I wasn't going to let anything stop me from getting out of there sooner than planned.

I was a mess of wires, tubes, drains, and cables in those first few days. Walking was hard enough due to the pain and my overall weakness, but I also had to make sure I didn't trip over all the tubes each time I got up and walked.

The NG (nasogastric) tube was supposed to stay in for at least a week. Because they had to remove part of my pancreas, intestine, and stomach to remove the tumor, there were concerns that my stomach wouldn't pump things through correctly, so I needed the NG tube to assist. But due to a slight mishap on my part, that NG tube didn't stay in for a week.

On the third day, I got up for one of my walks. As I tried to adjust the tubing connected to my IV pole, I somehow got tangled up and yanked the NG tube out of my nose. I'm not even sure how it actually happened. I panicked a little and called the nurse in to see how bad the situation was.

After she talked to the doctor, they decided they would just have to monitor and see how I responded. If my body didn't take over, they would have to reinstall the NG tube, which did not sound like a fun experience. Fortunately, my body responded well. At the very least, it was one less tube to get in the way during my walks.

I walked more and more, improving tenfold each day. On my fourth day, the nurses removed my pain pump. Once it was removed, the pain was still manageable. I was also able to start to take small sips of water and eat a little lemon ice.

Early on the fifth day, they removed my epidural. Still no setbacks. I continued to rack up laps around that hospital floor. Later that day, the nurse removed the drains. I was also able to eat a little bit of real food, if that's what you could call what they fed me. I was only allowed to eat three small bites at a time, as my body was not yet able to digest and process things correctly, but I was eating. My doctors started to talk about maybe letting me go home in the following days. We were way ahead of schedule now.

On the morning of day six, my nurses removed the final tubes, my catheter, and my IV. I was completely free! We were still trying to dial in the dosage of the medication that helped me digest food, CREON, but other than that everything was going great. After a little convincing on my part, they decided I was ready to be discharged. Six days after a more than thirteen-hour Whipple procedure I was sent home to recover—a full two weeks earlier than projected.

It felt like I had conquered another battle. My positive attitude and all that walking had led to my expedited discharge. I almost hugged the doctor when they agreed to let me go home, I was so excited. After receiving the discharge paperwork and changing out of the hospital gown that had been my outfit for the previous week, I was ready to go.

Katie was parked near the on-campus apartments where she'd been staying. I knew that it was going to be quite a long walk, but I declined the traditional wheelchair escort, thinking that a long walk seemed like the only appropriate way for me to leave. Walking had become my thing while there. I might as well walk my way out too.

So that's what we did. Katie and I, walking out together, holding hands. We walked through the entire hospital to get to the back exit that would lead us to her car. As I walked, I smiled happily at every doctor and nurse we passed. I was beaming with pride.

I felt like I had just completed a marathon. In a way, I guess I had. I'm not sure I can remember a time when I was more full of joy. I had of course been happy when originally finding out that Dr. K had been able to remove the tumor, but at that time, I was so focused on recovery and getting better so I could leave that the joy of the tumor being gone hadn't truly set in yet. But now, as we walked through the hospital corridors, the joy of it all hit me fully.

We entered the large courtyard between the hospital and the apartments. I had barely so much as looked out the window the previous six days. When the sunlight hit my face, it was blinding but glorious.

Something felt different. Maybe it was just the change in environment after the long hospital stay, but I truly believe the feeling I was having, the feeling that everything in my world was now more vivid and alive, was due to the miracle I had just received. The tumor that was never supposed to be removable was gone. That was a miracle. It made the sunlight on my face feel a little brighter. The air filling my lungs felt crisper than I can ever remember. The grass in the courtyard looked a little greener and smelled a little fresher than anything I could recall.

I paused briefly. I took a few very deep breaths. As my lungs filled with air, I felt a huge appreciation for everything, for life in general. As I stood there breathing deeply, I said a quick thank you to God for the miracle I had received.

With that, Katie and I walked happily across the courtyard to head home to our kids, back where we belonged.

CHAPTER 22

FINALLY CANCER-FREE—WHAT THE HELL DO I DO NOW?

Recovery at home continued relatively smoothly. For the most part, I was ahead of schedule. I continued my walks once at home, although they were still short at first. The weather was very nice for late fall, so I was able to enjoy those walks outside in the sun. At first, I could only walk a few homes down our street and back, but that changed quickly. On October 3, just a week and a half after my surgery, I was able to take a sun-filled, one-mile walk in the neighborhood. I did get a brief lecture from my at-home nurse/wife for overdoing it a little, but it felt good to achieve that milestone. I was again pushing the limits of what I was "supposed" to be able to do and loving every minute of it.

On October 5, I had my first postsurgical appointment with Dr. K. That appointment could not have gone much better. My incision was healing nicely. My body was recovering quicker than we could have hoped. Most importantly, the preliminary pathology report had come back and showed clear margins. Per the pathologist's analysis of the tumor, it was determined that it was mostly inactive.

There were minimal scattered active cancer cells, which indicated that all the chemotherapy and radiation over the previous two years had worked. Dr. K had removed nine lymph nodes during the surgery. None of them were positive for cancer.

Dr. K was as happy with the report as we were. When he uttered the words "cancer-free," I almost burst into tears. After over two years of fighting and praying, I was finally *cancer-free*. But Dr. K also made sure that we understood the high likelihood of the cancer returning at some point in the future. Up to 75 percent of pancreatic cancer patients have cancer recurrence postsurgery. When it comes to pancreatic cancer, it seems there is almost always some bad news to counterbalance any good news you receive. Our fight was not over. It would never be fully over. But for now, being cancer-free was the best news we could have hoped to receive.

The only significant issue after surgery was figuring out my diet and how to regain weight. I had lost twenty pounds since the surgery. Most of that loss was the result of the time in the hospital when I wasn't able to eat at all. Dr. K had told me that adjusting my diet and appetite after the Whipple was very similar to being a toddler again. I had to relearn what foods I liked and what foods I could best tolerate. Sometimes people who disliked or couldn't tolerate spicy foods prior to surgery loved them after, or vice-versa. I also had a smaller stomach post-surgery, so I had to ensure I consumed only smaller portions. This meant I had to have more meals daily than I was used to, but with much smaller portion sizes for each meal. I had to ascertain how and what to eat that best fit my new body.

It was all quite an adjustment, but I was adapting. Over time, I figured out what foods worked for me. Fortunately, I didn't have too many significant changes from my pre-surgery food preferences. There were a few things I could no longer tolerate, like leafy green vegetables, but for the most part it was manageable. Over time my portion sizes returned to normal. After a few months, my body even adjusted enough that I was able to mostly eliminate my need for the CREON.

I still struggled to gain significant weight. Considering what my body had gone through, having to live at a slightly lower weight wasn't that bad of an outcome all things considered. Heck, way back at the beginning of this journey, living at a slightly lower weight had actually been a goal, not something I considered a negative outcome.

I also struggled with adjusting my mental and emotional state after the surgery. In all honesty, my mental and emotional struggles far outweighed the physical. All I had known over the last two years was the fight. Fighting cancer had consumed everything else. I was a cancer warrior, and that had become my entire identity. Now I was cancer-free. What was I supposed to do with all that energy that had been focused completely on fighting cancer? What was my new identity supposed to be? Who was I if I wasn't a cancer warrior anymore?

It was also a struggle to accept that the cancer was really gone and not going to come back suddenly and rock our lives all over again. After having regular bloodwork, scans, and doctor appointments consistently, I was now on my own. I would no longer have those regular checkups multiple times a month to keep an eye on things. Now I just had to wait until my next scans, which would only occur three or four times a year going forward, and trust that the cancer was gone and hadn't snuck back somewhere new in my body.

That caused a whole new type of anxiety that I was trying to overcome. Every cough or sore muscle became a concern. Had the cancer returned, or did I just push a little too hard in yesterday's workout? Did I just have an upset stomach from something I ate, or was there a new tumor growing somewhere within my abdomen? This was a new mental battle I had to learn to manage.

Eventually, the same things that helped me with my cancer fight ended up helping alleviate these new concerns. I leaned hard into my faith and trust in God, pushed to always stay positive, and used my increasing number of workouts to relieve any new stress. I also had to learn to open up about these concerns with Katie more, and she was then able to help ease my mind and make me realize that the worst-case scenario wasn't my reality.

Three weeks after surgery, I rejoined our coaching staff on the sidelines to coach our Oxford Junior Wildcat football team in a game. I wasn't as active on the sidelines as normal right away, cautiously taking it a little easy, but I was there. And it was exactly what I needed. It made me feel like I was getting back to my normal life. I was able to coach the last three games of the season. Life was getting back to normal quicker than expected.

On October 20, I had my one-month postsurgical CT scan and follow-up appointment. My CT scan results were still completely clear, and I was still cancer-free. Dr. K told me that after reviewing my case and status with the tumor board, the team that evaluates and determines treatment plans, it was determined that I would not need to do any additional precautionary chemo going forward. I was done! I was now officially on an observation-only plan, meaning I would continue to have CT scans every three or four months for the rest of my life, but at the time I needed no additional treatment beyond that. This was the absolute best-case scenario.

Due to the extensive recovery required for such a major surgery, I was not allowed to start running again for six to eight weeks. I of course targeted the six-week mark, and six weeks to the day after my surgery, I ran for the first time. I was able to get a mile and a half in at a pretty good pace, considering my body was still not even close to fully recovered. It felt so good to be out doing what I loved again, running on that cool fall day. I was determined to get back to my pre-surgery distances and pace as quickly as possible.

I was going to fight through any hurdles and get back to as close to 100 percent as possible, as quickly as possible. Dr. K had told me before the surgery that it was likely that I would only ever get back to 90 percent of my normal self after the surgery. This was regarding energy, working out, and almost everything else. I was determined to prove him wrong, to be better than I was pre-surgery, in all those areas. I would be 150 percent of my former self.

In mid-November, exactly seven weeks after my surgery, I ran in a 5k race at our local park. I was running that race to prove that I could do anything, that nothing could slow me down. I not only ran the race; I ran it in a very competitive twenty-six-minute time! I was not yet back to my pre-surgery pace, but I was close. I was determined to take full advantage of this second chance I was given, and this race was another step in that direction.

The big question was, "What's next?"

First, I had to adapt to my new cancer-free, observation-only status. I had to learn to not let every little cough or pain freak me out. I had to learn to trust in the doctors and this new plan and continue to trust in God to guide me through it. It was a struggle at first. Refocusing on a life without cancer as the central point was difficult.

But the further I moved past surgery, the easier it became. I realized I couldn't live in a constant state of worry and what-ifs. The cancer might eventually come back, but I couldn't live life fearing that it would. I had to live for the moment, and I would deal with any future recurrence when and if it actually happened. Shifting my mindset was a challenge, but it was a shift I was able to make in time.

Next, I knew I had to find new outlets for all my energy. I knew I wanted, and needed, to find a way to give back. So many people had helped me in so many ways during my battle with cancer, and I knew I had to figure out how to help others in return. I started to formulate plans to do just that.

I found some speaking opportunities within my community that allowed me to tell my story and inspire others in similar fights. I also found some nonprofit cancer support organizations where

I was able to volunteer and become a mentor, giving me another avenue to help others in their cancer battles. Shortly after surgery, I volunteered to assist on a medical mission trip to Honduras with Katie and a team of medical professionals. I was so excited to have the opportunity to help with the great work that Katie and her fellow colleagues did for the people of Honduras.

While it was a challenge to shift my focus from the thing that had monopolized my entire life for the past few years, I was starting to figure it out. I was finding a new purpose. I was finding ways to give back. I was finding ways to become a better version of myself, the absolute best version of myself.

Being cancer-free was a blessing, a blessing that I planned to take full advantage of.

CHAPTER 23

MY STORY IS NOT YET FINISHED

Cancer never fully goes away. Once you've been diagnosed, it's something that you are stuck with forever. Even when it has been removed from your body, it never really disappears from your life. It is just a part of your being, forever.

The key to living with this new reality is acknowledging and accepting that fact but not letting it completely absorb you. Cancer may be a part of who you are forever after diagnosis, but it doesn't have to fully define you and determine how you live life. It doesn't have to be a bad thing. I once saw Stuart Scott reference a quote from Linda Ellis. "Your life is made up of two dates and a dash. Make the most of the dash." That's my plan. Cancer really makes you realize that no one is promised tomorrow. Not you, not me—none of us. You have to live for today. Each and every one of us should live the dash to the fullest. I plan to make my dash the greatest I possibly can for as long as I possibly can.

Cancer has made me a better person; it has made me stronger. Cancer has also made me more faithful and more positive. This horrible disease has made me appreciate all the wonderful people in my life so much more. It has made me appreciate all the small things and worry far less about what I thought were the important things like advancing in my career and filling our bank account. Cancer has made me more aware of the impact I can have on the world and gave me an endless desire to make that impact.

My faith is strong. I choose to believe that God gave me cancer for a reason. I must follow God's plan for me and ensure I bring some good to the world as a result of my battle. I also choose to believe that God's plan for me is to be cancer-free. I believe that God does not leave us in our trials and adversities forever. At some point He always brings us through that valley, in one way or another. But as Proverbs 3:5–6 says, "Trust in the Lord with all your heart, and lean not on your own understanding. . . ." It is not my job to understand His plan, whether that means cancer eventually returns or if it never does. It is only my job to trust His plan. After all, it is God's plan and not mine.

But I will choose to live life as if that plan is for me to remain cancer-free. If my cancer-free status does change at some point, then I will adjust and follow the same principles I have followed so far. My faith will get me through whatever is to come, whether that includes a cancer recurrence or just other life challenges. I am not going to go out easily. I will keep fighting and keep living life to its fullest for every minute I get. I will try to live every one of those minutes to make a positive impact on the lives of others. I will try to live completely for my family because they are my biggest "why."

The term "cancer warrior" is used quite frequently in the cancer community, and specifically by me as well. At first, that term felt awkward to me. The title of warrior felt more than I had earned. Most warriors choose their fight. A soldier enlists in the military and chooses to serve their country. A Navy Seal makes the difficult decision to go through BUD/S training and take on the most challenging of military professions. A boxer chooses to train himself endlessly to step into the ring and face his opponent. I didn't choose my battle. Cancer chose it for me.

I was forced into the fight. I did, however, choose how I responded to the enormous challenge cancer threw into my life. I chose to start fighting almost immediately after diagnosis, in those late-night hours in the hospital when that amazing little nurse gave me a little hope and boosted my faith. I picture that moment in the middle of the night in that uncomfortable hospital bed as a fork in the road. The path to the right was the warrior path. The path to the left was the victim path. That night, right at the beginning of my cancer journey, I chose the warrior path.

I chose to fight, and to fight hard. I chose to give every ounce of energy I had in my battle against cancer. I guess I earned the warrior title at that point, at the very start of my battle, simply by choosing to fight for my life. I chose to fight for myself. I chose to fight for my family. I chose to fight for my friends. I chose to train myself physically, mentally, emotionally, and spiritually for my battle with cancer, similar to the way soldiers and Navy Seals and MMA fighters train themselves for their battles. The choice to fight is what earned me—and so many others like me—the title of cancer warrior.

I had similar feelings about the term "bravery" as I did about the term "warrior." People have often said throughout my battle, "You are so brave. I don't know if I could do what you have." Statements like this make it sound like I had a choice. When I think of a brave person, I think of a guy running into a burning building to save the kids (like in the movie *The Outsiders*). That person chose to put his life at risk, running into the fire instead of running away.

I was thrown into the fire; I didn't run in by choice. But I did have a choice in how I responded, and I chose to respond bravely. I chose to never give up, and to fight like hell. That response was a choice. To me, being a brave warrior simply means to make a choice to throw everything you have (physically, mentally, emotionally, and spiritually) into your battle or challenge. That is exactly what I have done. Everyone can do that in their own challenges as well if they choose their own warrior path and avoid the victim path.

Some people have also asked me if I am apprehensive at all in using the terms "survived cancer" or "beat cancer." I use those terms fairly regularly, but not in any way lightly. I do not use those terms to imply my fight with cancer is over. It will never be over. I have no false pretenses that the cancer won't ever come back. The pancreatic cancer recurrence rate for patients who undergo the Whipple procedure is around 75 percent, so it very likely will return at some point. There's a very good chance that it will ultimately kill me.

But that doesn't mean I haven't survived it or beat it. In his famous Jimmy V Perseverance Award acceptance speech at the 2014 ESPYs, while in the midst of the worst of his battle with cancer, Stuart Scott said, "When you die, that does not mean that you lose to cancer. You beat cancer by how you live, why you live, and in the manner in which you live." That is how I have beaten cancer. That is how I will continue to beat cancer. I will live life to its absolute fullest, and I will never let cancer determine my "how" or my "why." By doing that, cancer can never beat me. I will always win. I will always survive.

Going forward, I will focus on applying what I coached to so many of my players. Control the things you have control over, the most important of those things being your attitude and your effort. Attitude and effort are choices. We should all choose to have a positive attitude. We should all choose to give 100 percent in everything. None of us can be positive and give 100 percent effort all the time, each and every day. But, if we keep it as a focus, keep coming back to it, we can ensure we get the benefits of that positive attitude and effort more days than not.

Focusing on my attitude and my effort served me well in my cancer fight. And I know it will continue to serve me well in any future life challenges. So, I will continue to apply what I have coached. I will fight off the negative and strive to be a positive light. I will give everything I have in everything I do.

As much as I love numbers and statistics, I've loved defying the statistics even more. I've found so much joy in beating the odds. Getting out of the hospital in four days after my first Whipple instead of the projected ten made me so happy. Getting out of the hospital in six days instead of the projected twenty after my second Whipple made me proud. Being one of the less than 1 percent to get two chances at a Whipple made me a unicorn of sorts, and I love that. Running a 5k seven weeks after my second Whipple was extremely unlikely, but I did it. Heck, just being alive three years after diagnosis has defied all the odds. There were so many things that I was able to do during my cancer fight that were highly improbable, if not impossible. But all those things made me realize that nothing is impossible. With a little faith, a lot of hard work, the right support system, and the right attitude, any of us can do anything.

So, while the odds of my cancer coming back someday are pretty high, I don't worry about it. Maybe I completely beat the odds again and it never returns. Maybe I'm a unicorn in that way also.

Or maybe it does come back at some point. If it does, I know what to do. I know how to fight it. I will once again defy the odds, and kick cancer's ass.

Prior to my cancer, I lived life going 900 miles per hour. I tried to do everything, often all at once. Career, family, hobbies, pretty much every part of my life I pushed to excessive speeds. I wanted it all, and I wanted it immediately. At first, cancer made me want to go even faster. I felt I didn't have enough time left on the clock, and that I had to squeeze it all in as quickly as possible. But then it started to have the opposite impact.

I started to slow down. I started to appreciate things more—all things. I started to really and truly stop and smell the roses. I finally began to appreciate everything, as I should have all along. The joy of the sun hitting my face, a nice breeze on a run, the happiness I felt hearing my kids giggle, and the delight of seeing Katie's smile all began to mean so much more to me.

None of us are promised tomorrow. Cancer makes you very aware of that. It makes you really appreciate the important stuff and disregard all the noise in the world. That is a lesson too many people never learn. Since cancer slapped me in the face with this lesson, I plan to take full advantage of it. I plan to embrace the important stuff with both arms. I plan to make an impact. I have always wanted to find ways to help and serve others more, but never found the avenue or push to make it happen to any significance. Cancer is that push.

Having a wife like mine who has built a career around helping others is awesome. But as awesome as it is to have a wife who does so many amazing things that help so many people, it also can make you feel a little less than. I have struggled for years to find the meaning in what I do. I'm an executive in the auto industry. I sell software to big corporations to put in cars that they sell to the public. It's hard to find the big-picture value in that sometimes. I have a wife who literally saves people's lives, while I am selling software buried deep in a car that most people don't know exists or care about unless something doesn't function right on their daily commute.

I have long felt I needed to do more. I am a loving and caring person, and really feel I have so much more to give. Cancer made me feel this deep down in my heart, even more than I did before. But cancer puts a time limit on everything. You can no longer say, "Oh, I'll get to that someday." Cancer makes you realize that your future somedays might be a lot less than you had hoped. It gives you urgency.

I'm on a mission to serve others like never before. There's no time to waste. Before Dr. K had even removed my tumor, I had already started helping others in their fight with cancer by volunteering for

Imerman Angels, a cancer peer-to-peer support nonprofit. I will do whatever necessary to help as many cancer warriors in need as possible, as so many helped me when I was in the worst of my fight.

Shortly after my surgery, I also had the opportunity to tell my story to one of our local sports teams in an effort to inspire and motivate them, to show them that they can overcome any challenge through hard work and with the right attitude. Speaking opportunities like that are another incredible way for me to give back, to help others, to inspire. I have an amazing story, a story that thankfully is not yet finished. My story can encourage, motivate, and inspire many. So, I will tell it every chance I get.

I am also giving back through other volunteer opportunities, like my mission trip to Honduras. The nonprofit Katie and I run is focused completely on providing healthcare to those who don't have the necessary access to it. Mission trips are a key part of our organization's objectives. Prior to cancer, I struggled to find time to join Katie on those mission trips. Again, cancer changed that as well. It's now a priority, something I happily make time for.

I love coaching. It's a key part of my identity and one of my most valuable skills. I will continue to coach the kids in our community.

I hope this book is helpful to some. I hope it inspires a few. I hope it gives a little hope to many. For me, it was extremely therapeutic to write. It helped me come to grips with how cancer has affected and changed me. Writing it was beneficial to me and has helped me to grow. But that's not why I wrote it. I strongly feel God gave me cancer for a reason. Part of that reason has to be for me to use my cancer battle and story for good. To help others. To inspire. To give hope. I sincerely feel this book is part of God's plan for me. So I hope, at a minimum, it helped you in some small way. Hopefully it inspired you, at least a little. And hopefully it gave you some hope that the most challenging of fights can be won.

When I was first diagnosed, I started looking for books to help me understand my new cancer life. At first, I read more scientific, medically focused books in an effort to learn what I was in for. But I realized that wasn't what I wanted. I needed a book to inspire me and give me hope. Once I realized what I was looking for, I found many that became critical in my fight.

First, I read Stuart Scott's *Every Day I Fight: Making a Difference, Kicking Cancer's Ass*. I actually started reading it while still in the hospital after the biopsy where I learned of my cancer. That book may have saved me. It inspired me so much. It gave me hope and made me want to fight. It laid the groundwork for my battle.

Next, I read a book by a pancreatic cancer survivor named Steven Lewis. The book was called *The Ripple Effect: How a Positive Attitude and a Caring Community Helped Save My Life*. That book reinforced my belief that a positive attitude would be critical in my fight.

The next book that helped inspire me in my fight was *What It Takes: Fighting for My Life and My Love of the Game* by Mark Herzlich, the former Boston College and New York Giants football player who overcame a battle with bone cancer. All three of these books, and multiple others, helped me. My hope is that this book can provide you just a little of what those books did for me.

I will finish by reiterating the six-part strategy that was critical for me in my battle with pancreatic cancer.

1. Faith.
2. A positive attitude.
3. A focus on what I was fighting for.
4. Fitness and my physical health.
5. A strong support system.
6. Advocating for my own health plan.

Those pillars have carried me through the most challenging struggle of my life. I've survived my fight. Through that battle, I was able to grow into a better person. I fought, I survived, and I eventually thrived. My story is not yet finished. I feel the best is yet to come. I plan to completely enjoy every single moment along the way!

#FaithOverFear

AUTHOR'S NOTE

ADVOCATING FOR YOUR OWN
HEALTH PLAN

Being diagnosed with cancer is overwhelming. It's scary to begin with, but then you are bombarded with so many choices of healthcare systems, doctors, and treatment plans. I think it's just too much for many in the fight, and they just accept whatever's presented to them first.

Cancer is not a simple thing. It's critical that each of us fighting cancer takes control, advocates for what's best for each of us, and finds the best fit of doctors and treatments possible. There's nothing more important than having the healthcare plan that fits our individual needs, and the only way we can ensure we get that is to strongly advocate for ourselves.

I was lucky. Prior to being diagnosed, I met Dr. A while in the hospital with my liver bile leak, and I knew from very early on that Dr. A's personality and proposed course of treatment was a good fit for me. I wasn't given just a standard plan; Dr. A and her team developed the most aggressive plan possible, largely based on my young age and good health and fitness levels, to give me the best chance of not just extending life, but a plan that gave me the best chance to become cancer-free someday.

Dr. A and her team were the perfect fit for me. I not only loved Dr. A—I loved her entire staff. The infusion center nurses, the front office staff, and her nurse practitioner were all an ideal fit for my needs. Not only did all our personalities mesh well, but they also put in significant effort to adapt treatments and anything else necessary to my specific needs to make things as easy as possible. Having them as my team gave me one less thing to worry about. I was able to just trust them and focus on getting better. Finding that perfect team is the first and most important step in ensuring you get the best healthcare plan and strategy that fits you specifically.

I was with that team for the entire duration of my cancer. But I eventually needed to find a new surgeon to make a second attempt. My first surgeon was not willing to make a second surgical attempt, so my only hope was to find someone new who would be willing to at least try. I began searching and found Dr. K at another large metro Detroit cancer center. When I found him online, I somehow knew immediately he was the right surgeon. I felt it deep in my heart. I truly believed God led me to him, and that he was who I needed to see. As time went on, I realized just how right I was about that feeling. Once I met him in person, my feelings that he was the right fit were completely validated. From that point on, I had two healthcare teams supporting me in the fight: my initial team at the first cancer institute, plus my new surgical oncology team at a different one. I trusted my instincts and put my full faith in both of those teams. If needed, I would have found a third team. I would pursue whatever was needed to give me the best chance of beating cancer.

Beyond finding the right healthcare team, I strongly believe we also need to pursue as many additional options as possible. I am a firm believer that mainstream medicine, including chemotherapy, radiation, and surgical intervention, is necessary as the primary method for fighting cancer. But I also felt I needed to remain open to other additional actions that may help. There are many herbal supplements that many people believe help our bodies fight against cancer. They are mostly sold as over-the-counter medications, and most have no significant side effects. Some examples are turmeric, moringa, Vitamin C (intravenously), Vitamin D, Vitamin E, milk thistle, ginger root, and many others. There are not many official studies to prove their effectiveness against cancer, but there are also typically no negative effects in trying them. For me, many of these supplements made me feel better and gave me more energy, so were worth taking.

I did my best to continuously research the latest and greatest in publications and clinical trials for pancreatic cancer. In today's world, things are changing constantly with cancer research and discoveries. There is new information released almost daily. For my grandparents' generation, being diagnosed with cancer, especially pancreatic cancer, meant almost certain death. And it typically meant a quick death. But that's no longer the case. Thanks to the significant cancer research being done by organizations such as the American Cancer Institute and the V Foundation, cancer can be survivable, and it becomes more so every year. These amazing organizations are finding cures. We need to continue to donate and support them so that the research can continue, and cancer can become curable in every case.

But typically, no one is going to place the research findings or new clinical trial options right in your lap. You need to take ownership of your own fight, do your research, and find those new opportunities for treatment and actively pursue them. Again, you need to own your care. You need to find your own options. When clinical trials became available, I would always research it, and then discuss it with my oncology team to see if it was an option for me. There are new clinical trial options coming out all the time, so researching and investigating what could work for my situation became a critical regular activity to ensure I was pursuing any and all options for the best cancer care possible.

I also tried two other alternative methods that I felt helped, although I have no way of proving how effective they really were. I added regular cold showers and hot saunas to my weekly routine. I had read that there was anecdotal evidence that both hot and cold therapy could help with cancer survival.

Shortly after my diagnosis, we added an infrared sauna to our home gym in the basement. I began using that regularly throughout my treatments. When I was struggling to be active at all, I was able to use the sauna to at least elevate my heart rate (similar to a workout) while also sweating out some of the toxins in my body. I also finished my showers by turning the water as cold as it would go for the last few minutes of my shower. It was shocking but gave me an energy boost and made me feel better overall. The combination of extreme cold therapy with my showers and extreme heat therapy in the sauna seemed to help in my recovery. Regardless of its impact on the cancer, both therapy methods made me feel better in general and, I believe, had a positive impact on my body.

When I was first diagnosed, everything came at me so fast I felt like I was just along for the ride. "Chemo? Radiation? Sure, whatever you guys tell me to do is fine." But as I started to get more into the fight, I took more ownership of things. I realized I had a say in my treatment plans, a say in who treated me, and a say in if I wanted to pursue additional, nontraditional methods to help me in the battle. It was my battle, after all. I chose to own it and advocate for myself as I went through the fight.

ACKNOWLEDGMENTS

Gratitude has become a central focus for me since cancer came into my life. I truly have so much to be thankful for. I am so grateful to so many people who have helped me both in my fight against cancer and also in the writing of this memoir. The writing of this book has further helped me to appreciate just how lucky I am to be surrounded by so many amazing people. So I can think of no better way to wrap this thing up than to thank some of the many people who were so instrumental in making it happen.

First and foremost, I must thank God! Not only is He my ultimate healer who carried me through my entire cancer battle and allowed me to survive what many thought was unsurvivable, but He also blessed me with all the tools necessary to endure every struggle cancer threw my way.

There is absolutely zero chance that I would have survived cancer or been able to complete the writing of this memoir without my incredible family. Above all, I have to thank my beautiful wife, Katie. She is my rock. She was the world's best cancer caregiver and my guide through my entire battle. She pushed me when I needed to be pushed and picked me up when I couldn't move forward without assistance. She also supported me 100 percent when I came to her with the crazy idea of publishing a book documenting my journey. I thank God every day for blessing me with her as my perfect partner.

Next, I have to thank my four children: Tristen, Landon, Parker, and Grady. You guys are my motivation and inspiration for everything. You were the only thing that could keep me in the fight in the worst of it. The fear of not being here to see all the amazing things you do and will do in the future drove me to keep grinding with everything I had in me. My fight was for you, and this book is as well.

To the rest of my family, you are truly the most amazing family ever. There was never a time when Katie and the kids and I felt as if we were fighting the cancer monster alone. We had you, our beloved army of family, behind us and carrying us through it all. There is not a big enough thank you possible for my parents (Cindy and Dan), Katie's parents (Vonda and Kevin), my brother Ryan and his family, Katie's siblings Casey and Dana and their families, and all the cousins, aunts and uncles, nieces and nephews, and grandparents who are the greatest team I have ever been a part of.

Beyond family, I have also been blessed with friends who are like family. Covering them all here would take pages, but I need to acknowledge some of you for sure. Kevin and Danielle and Mike and Dawn; we met as neighbors, but I could not be more thankful that our relationship grew into family. To my "224 River" boys (Clayton, Joel, and Matt), you guys are my brothers. From the first day of college to the last day of my life you have been and always will be the first guys I go to, so keep that group text open and ready always. Alistair, my Scottish brother, thank you for always answering the phone for my vent sessions and for always being such a good listener and friend. Al and Sara, you were the first people I told after diagnosis, and you immediately jumped into the role of my motivational team. Thank you; you helped get me up off the mat and into the fight. Thank you to all the guys I coached alongside in lacrosse, basketball, and football. You guys helped me to shift focus away from my struggles and on to the sports I love and the kids we love coaching. Thanks to all my current and former players, as well as all their parents. My players inspired me. They showed me how to scrap. They also gave me so much joy by seeing the happiness the sports I so love gave them. The parents supported me, and I appreciate them trusting me to coach their amazing kids over the years. A huge thank you to all of my former coaches and teammates who taught me how to battle at an early age. To my amazing Oxford community, thank you all. Oxford is a community that always steps up huge for any of our own in need. When that was me, you were there for me. Thanks for that. A big thank you to all my friends in my hometown of Muskegon, Michigan. You've been there with me since the beginning, and you remained right by my side through all my struggles. I must, of course, also thank all my Facebook prayer warriors! Your consistent prayers, comments, and messages picked me up more times than you will ever know. I firmly believe in the power of prayer and know that the power of your prayers played a huge part in me still being here today.

I next have to thank all my fellow cancer warriors. There is a special bond amongst those of us who have experienced the challenges of facing cancer. It is a bond that ties us tightly together, in a way that few can relate to. To those special warriors from the infusion center who sat by my side for so many treatment days, thank you. I do not miss sitting in that chair one bit, but I do miss sitting next to all of you. To my buddy Tate, thanks for all of the inspiration and motivation. I can't wait to watch all the amazing things you will do in this world. To all my friends who have also battled cancer, thank you for being there for me with the understanding that only those who have also been through the fight can have. To my fellow mentors and my mentees in Imerman Angels, thank you for being amazing cancer peers and friends. Thank you to the Imerman Angels organization for creating such an amazing peer-to-peer mentoring community. You found a way to provide exactly what us cancer patients and survivors need and are a blessing to us all. A special thanks to my mother-in-law/second mom, Vonda, for showing me how to be a cancer warrior before I ever knew I would need that knowledge as she battled so gracefully through her battle with breast cancer years before my fight. You kicked its ass and showed me the way. As all of us warriors are tied together, I want to thank each and every person around the world who has fought their own cancer battle. Every single cancer story I have ever heard has inspired me along the way. Each of you has your own story, all of which are inspiring and motivating. So thank you, my fellow cancer warriors, and remember, we are all in this together—always!

I of course have to thank all the amazing medical teams who cared for me throughout my cancer journey. First and foremost, a huge thank you to my first oncologist, Dr. A, and her incredible team. She was always caring and empathetic, and exuded a confidence that we could beat my cancer as a team. Her demeanor gave me hope when I needed it the most. Her team, specifically my nurse practitioner Jen and nurses Sherri and Casey, literally kept me alive at the beginning of my fight, and somehow also found a way to always bring joy to my days, making me smile when smiles were hard to come by. Dr. K, the oncology surgeon who removed my tumor via a Whipple procedure in September of 2022, quite literally saved my life. His confidence in his incredible surgical abilities and his compassion for a guy who wasn't quite ready to leave this world yet propelled him to take a chance that others were not willing to take. I likely wouldn't be here today if that weren't the case. God put Dr. K in my life with a purpose, and I thank both God and Dr. K for that every day. I must also thank Dr. K's amazing team, specifically his nurse practitioner, Tanya, for the incredible care they have continued to give me over the years since my surgery. I also need to thank my radiation oncologist Dr. F, whose awesome care and hilarious sense of humor made going through radiation seem not quite so bad. To the unknown nurse who gave me so much hope by praying over me on that first night after diagnosis, thank you. You unknowingly set the course for my fight and in many ways, even beyond cancer, saved my life. There are so many other incredible nurses, nurse practitioners, CT and MRI techs, and other oncology and hospital staff members who had a positive impact on me during my battle. They rarely get the recognition that they so deserve as they diligently care for so many people like me who are fighting for their lives. They make our struggles more manageable and truly are angels to all of us. Thank you to each and every one of you!

A huge thank you to all my colleagues and coworkers for the support you gave me while I went through my cancer journey. My colleagues at both Argus and Continental made it possible for me to continue my career and do what I love despite the added challenges of my cancer. I must specifically thank my CEO at Argus, Ronen, for his amazing leadership and support of my family after I was diagnosed. Thank you to all of you; you are more than coworkers to me; you are friends who I just happen to work with.

Thank you to Gina and her team at New Day Foundation, who helped my family find the resources we needed at our most difficult time.

Finally, I must thank the team that made this book possible. Without the expertise and professionalism of the amazing team at KN Literary Arts, there is zero chance that I could have pushed this memoir to the finish line. A huge thank you to Jennifer Sanders, who guided me through the process like a champion, and also made me smile every time we talked. Kelly Bergh, thank you for your incredible patience and editing abilities as you expertly pulled content out of this inexperienced author's head. You are an editor extraordinaire. Thank you to Erin Seaward-Hiatt, whose creativity as a designer gave me a beautiful-looking book that I am so proud of. Thank you to my good friend Rae Jean Erickson for the cover and author photo; you are truly the best. Finally, thank you to the person who guided me through this process from day one. My book guru and awesome friend, Amy Hosford. Your guidance made this book possible. Beyond making it possible, you made the process of creating it enjoyable. You are a true light to the world. Thank you for being there from start to finish!

Again, thank you all so much for all you have done to support me both through my cancer battle and through the writing of this memoir. I love you all so much!

ABOUT DUSTY MYSEN

Born on August 1, 1973, in Muskegon, Michigan, **Dusty Mysen** grew up surrounded by his family and friends along the shores of Lake Michigan. He graduated from Michigan State University in 1995 with a bachelor's degree in electrical engineering. Following college, Dusty embarked on a fulfilling career spanning various roles within the automotive industry. Dusty has always been deeply rooted in family values. Together with his wife, Katie, they have raised four wonderful children: Tristen, Landon, Parker, and Grady.

In September 2020, at the age of forty-seven, Dusty's life took an unexpected turn with a diagnosis of pancreatic cancer. This profound battle not only tested his resilience but also transformed him into a better person. His memoir, a testament to his journey and the challenges he faced, is his first literary endeavor, offering readers an intimate glimpse into his fight against cancer and the lessons learned along the way.

Printed in the USA
CPSIA information can be obtained
at www.ICGtesting.com
CBHW032049021224
18324CB00004B/5